S0-AYD-497

MOVING OUT, MOVING UP

Families Beyond Shelter

ALSO BY RALPH DA COSTA NUNEZ

Beyond the Shelter Wall: Homeless Families Speak Out
A Shelter Is Not a Home . . . Or Is It?
The American Family Inn Handbook: A How-To Guide
The New Poverty: Homeless Families in America
Hopes, Dreams, & Promise: The Future of Homeless Children in America
Voyage to Shelter Cove
Saily's Journey
Cooper's Tale
Our Wish

Nunez, Ralph da Costa

Moving out, moving up

DATE DUE

Demco No. 62-0549

MOVING O

Families

Ralph

President of

Jesse

Foreword by
Leonard N. Stern
Founder of Homes for the Homeless

WHITE TIGER PRESS • NEW YORK

Library of Congress Cataloging-in-Publication Data

Cover photography: Todd Flashner
Cover design: James E. Farnum

ISBN 0-9724425-4-5

© 2006 Homes for the Homeless, Inc.
White Tiger Press
32A Cooper Square, New York, NY 10003

212-529-5252

www.whitetigerpress.com

A White Tiger Book

All rights reserved

No part of this book may be reproduced, stored in a retrieval system, or transmitted in any form, by any means, including electronic, mechanical, photocopying, microfilming, recording or otherwise, without prior written permission from the publisher.

Printed in the United States of America

This book is dedicated to service providers everywhere,
who make these success stories possible every day.
Thank you.

CONTENTS

FOREWORD

Moving Out, Moving Up is the second in a two-part series of books portraying the individual stories of men and women who have gone through the New York City shelter system. The first, *Beyond the Shelter Wall: Homeless Families Speak Out,*[1] highlighted the many causes of homelessness: teen pregnancies, domestic violence, and foster care, among others. But *Beyond the Shelter Wall* leaves one wondering if there is any real hope to ending homelessness. *Moving Out, Moving Up* answers that question. It shows the other side of homelessness, portraying the success stories that arise when young men and women are given the basic tools they need to succeed.

But it is also indirectly the story of the Homes for the Homeless American Family Inns, a different kind of shelter that we first opened almost twenty years ago. Our goal was to afford homeless families a chance to turn a shelter stay into a moment of opportunity, a chance to move from a sordid past to a promising future. *Moving Out, Moving Up* is a testament to that mission. Today we operate five Family Inns in New York City, housing over 600 families with over 1,200 children on any given day. Since our

1. Nunez, Ralph. *Beyond the Shelter Wall: Homeless Families Speak Out.* New York: White Tiger Press, 2004.

inception, over 29,000 families and 51,000 children have been served, and our work goes on.

While it is true that homelessness has become a more permanent fixture on the poverty landscape, these stories show that it can be overcome. Lives can change for the better. Dreams can come true. And children can reap the promise of a good education, a permanent home, and the opportunities they bring to their future. As you read the stories that follow, you will see just how that has happened for six particular families. It is our hope that their experiences will serve as a vanguard for the tens of thousands of others who face the challenges of family homelessness every day.

Leonard N. Stern
February 2006
New York City

ACKNOWLEDGEMENTS

Millions of families in America today are in the same or similar situations as were the families described in this book.[1] Many do not have access to the variety of services that allowed these families to overcome the problems they faced and become successful, contributing members of society. Shelly, Belle, Angela, Andre, Theresa, and Monique's willingness to share their stories allows us to spread this message to the decision-makers who are in a position to help others like them. This book is the result of the generosity of our interview subjects and without them, none of it would have been possible.

I must also extend my immense gratitude to the hardworking staff at the Institute for Children and Poverty in New York City. Special thanks go to my research assistant, Jesse Andrews Ellison, for her exceptional effort, conducting many hours of personal interviews and handling many editorial changes. Thanks also go to Laura Caruso, Robyn Schwartz, Jenny Yelin, Ryan Galvin, and Dona Anderson for reading each chapter numerous times and offering invaluable comments.

And most of all, a special thanks to all the staff of Homes

1. Burt, Martha R. 2001. *What Will It Take To End Homelessness?* Urban Institute. 1 October. http://www.urban.org/url.cfm?ID=310305 (Accessed Januray 9, 2006).

for the Homeless, especially the Administrators of the Family Inns, who work each day on the front lines of poverty. They are the ones who provide the inspiration and who serve as role models in leading young families out of homelessness and into independent, productive lives. Without their efforts none of the personal success stories in this book would have been possible. Thank you all.

Ralph da Costa Nunez
February 2006
New York City

INTRODUCTION

Today there are more shelters across America than at any time in recent history, and their numbers continue to grow. In the wake of Hurricane Katrina, family homelessness was thrust into the spotlight, but those of us who work with families living in poverty know that natural disasters are not the exclusive cause of displacement and homelessness. Family homelessness is a problem that has existed for decades, and organizations like Homes for the Homeless have been serving such families for nearly as long.

The six stories that follow are individual tales of struggle, survival, and eventual success. Each is unique, but together they represent the many thousands of families that pass through the New York City shelter system annually and, likewise, the millions of Americans who find themselves homeless every year. More than anything else, these stories demonstrate that if given the right tools and opportunities the transition from transience to stability, homelessness to housing, and dependence to self-sufficiency is possible.

The stories presented in *Moving Out, Moving Up* illustrate the range of factors that can lead to family homelessness—incomplete education, unexpected pregnancies, addiction, abuse, economic downturns, and incarceration.

1

These individuals are profoundly different, their struggles decidedly unique. Yet their stories converge and lives change for the better in what some might consider an unlikely place: a New York City homeless shelter. Some people might argue that a shelter is not a home. But with very little low income housing being built and the number of shelters expanding, more and more families are finding a shelter, at least for the time being, is in fact their home.

Today's shelters are worlds away from the congregate facilities that many associate with the homelessness crisis. While some city shelters are still emergency way-stations where families idle away their days, others have transformed into bustling communities where families participate in an array of educational, employment, or life-skills programs that provide them with the tools to succeed in society. These facilities have become new communities, communities of opportunity from which parents go to work and children to school, and where families are able to eventually achieve self-sufficiency and move on to other communities of permanent housing and independence.

It takes a community to end homelessness, and shelters have become communities where many powerful, positive changes can happen. Above all, these stories show that homelessness is not just about housing. How families enter the shelter system is one thing, but how they leave is another. From a transitional shelter, countless families are able to take their first steps out of poverty, because after all, the end of homelessness can begin at the shelter door.

EDITOR'S NOTE

The following chapters were compiled from one-on-one interviews conducted in 2004 and 2005. Six formerly homeless individuals were chosen and their interviews were recorded and transcribed. The quotes within these chapters are always attributed to the individual whose story is being told. Names and certain details have been changed to protect each individual's anonymity.

CHAPTER ONE
Shelly

Breaking an Intergenerational Cycle of Homelessness

I have people all the time tell me, "You are stubborn, you are hard-headed," which I am. I don't want to be overpowered. I'm stubborn, I'm very hard to break. I have to be that way.

Shelly saw the inside of the Emergency Assistance Unit (EAU) before she saw the inside of a school, but her experience is sadly typical for many of New York City's poorest families.[1] A childhood marked by transience, homelessness, time in foster care, a mentally ill single mother, and too many mouths and not enough money perpetuated an intergenerational cycle of poverty and dependence. But Shelly's story is remarkable—today, she works six days a week as an office manager for a local construction company, takes evening classes at a community college, volunteers with the local police force, and lives in a comfortable two-bedroom apartment in Harlem. Perhaps most remarkably, Shelly says "the shelter system made me a stronger person." She was incredibly generous with this project, willing to dedicate hours to interviews,

1. The Emergency Assistance Unit is the gateway to the City shelter system.

and openly re-hash painful and personal childhood memories, all so that she might help other women in similar positions.

A Fractured Family

Given the circumstances surrounding Shelly's upbringing, her own journey through the shelter system is hardly surprising. Born and raised in New York City, Shelly is the third of six daughters. Her mother, Beth, struggled with bipolar disorder and was unable to maintain long-term employment, which proved detrimental to the family. Shelly contends that her mother was very intelligent: "It's like she wasted it. She could have put it to good use," but she's sympathetic to her mother's illness and understandably hesitant to place judgment on her parenting. "I don't consider her to be a bad mother; I do consider her to be unfit. I feel that more of us would have succeeded if she would have done more."

Shelly's mother never married, and Shelly had no consistent father figure in the home while she and her sisters were growing up. Only two of Beth's six daughters—Shelly and her sister Candace—have the same father. Shelly's mother maintained strict rules for herself when it came to allowing men into a house filled with young girls. "There were relationships, but they were always outside of the home. If she became pregnant, we knew who the father was, but they never lived in our home."

Although Shelly and Candace share a biological father, Steven, Shelly has little contact with him and she doubts whether he is really her father. "Honestly, I just don't think this man is my father. But I guess my mother's going to take it to her grave." She suspects that Steven is unconvinced of his paternal status as well.

The two do not look biologically related, whereas Candace and Steven share common physical traits. Throughout Shelly's childhood, and even today, Steven has been significantly closer to Candace than he is to Shelly. In fact, he has yet to meet Shelly's two children, his grandchildren.

Today, Shelly accepts her limited contact with him. "At this point, I don't even care anymore. What difference is it going to make? I'm 26. He missed basically all of my life." Yet even as Shelly appears to be stubbornly resolute about her independence, she admits to a certain degree of hurt over her father's absence. "I guess he attempted to bring something [for Candace to give to Shelly's children]. I told my sister, 'Give him the address so he can come by and see the kids.' He never got the address. I just left it at that. I'm not going to beat myself in the head. What's done is done. You're a man. I was your responsibility. . . . I have moved on. There's nothing that I can say or do."

Homelessness and Foster Care

By the time that Shelly was five, her mother had given birth to four of what would be six daughters; Beth was single, unemployed, and under tremendous financial strain. When Shelly was five, her mother voluntarily placed her and her sisters in foster care. "I guess my mother got too overwhelmed." The girls were split up, and Shelly and her younger sister were sent to a foster family in Brooklyn. Unfortunately, Shelly's new foster family was abusive, far from an improvement over her mother's home. Some of the abuse was extreme: "My foster mother took my sister's hands and set them in fire. My sister had third degree burns." Since the girls had been voluntarily placed in foster care, rather than taken, when their foster mother's abuse was revealed, they were sent back to their mother.

But Beth still was not able to care for her children, so she sent Shelly and her younger sister to live with their aunt, Kathy, in New Jersey. While Shelly hesitates to call her aunt abusive in the same way as her previous foster parent, Kathy was incredibly strict and would beat the girls for relatively small infractions. "We got punished for simple things, like play-fighting and stuff like that. And they beat my sister ridiculously, really just ridiculously. I'm going to be honest, my aunt is a hypocrite and she is cruel."

After nearly two years away from their mother, Beth decided to take the children back. Now pregnant for the fifth time, Beth picked up Shelly, now in second grade, and her younger sister and brought them back to New York City. They went straight to the EAU.

Shelly has trouble recalling the exact amount of time her family spent in a shelter that time. She estimates that it was about a year, after which the family was placed in an apartment in Manhattan. They lived there for three years, until the building became uninhabitable because of a serious rodent infestation. "We was doing alright, up until sixth grade. In sixth grade we became homeless again because a rat jumped on the table while we were sitting there eating. It snatched a sandwich and ran away." Shelly's mother decided that the apartment was unacceptable for young children and returned to the EAU. "I mean, the rats were literally climbing into bed with us at this point and stealing the food. My mother said, 'Let's go.' And we went to EAU."

The family spent another year in a shelter before being placed in an apartment in Harlem. Shelly would stay there for eight years, up until the time she gave birth to her own daughter.

Teen Motherhood

While the family was now in permanent housing, they still faced daily struggles. For one thing, they had very little money. Beth was not receiving public assistance,[2] and the family was subsisting on a very limited income—the survivor benefits that Shelly's youngest sister, Brittany, had been receiving since her father's death.[3] As a result, Shelly dropped out of school when she was seventeen to help support the family. "I dropped out early, but I never had any problem in school. I was always a straight-A student. There were just a lot of family complications and stuff, so I had to quit school. My mom was struggling. There was no help, so I had to get a job to help."

Shelly got a job at a sandwich shop in the city and around the same time, she began seeing a childhood friend, Aaron, with whom she eventually became sexually active. "We were best friends. You know, we became intimate friends. We started dating. And when I became pregnant, he didn't want to be a father. And I didn't want to have an abortion. So I'm stuck between a rock and a hard place. He wanted to let me be pregnant and date other women. So I let him go." At 18, Shelly gave birth to her first child, a daughter she named Anastasia.

2. Public assistance and welfare are used interchangeably; both refer to the federal entitlement program Temporary Assistance for Needy Families (TANF).
3. Brittany's father had passed away, and she received approximately $500 per month in survivor benefits.

Throughout Shelly's teen years, her mother continued to struggle not only with the family finances but also with her own mental health. She tried to commit suicide three times while Shelly was a teenager. "She overdosed on pills when I was about seventeen. She [also] drank bleach and ammonia. So now, if my mother gets too overwhelmed with certain things, she has to be hospitalized, because she's basically a threat to herself."

The other children faced health problems as well. Brittany suffered from chronic asthma, which had gotten so severe she was often unable to leave the family's apartment. "Her asthma was so bad, she was allergic to trees; she was allergic to air; she was allergic to roaches. She was allergic to basically everything. Brittany couldn't go to school every day. Brittany would get a block away; she would catch an asthma attack. My mother would have to bring her back, put her on the machine. My mother asked for home schooling. They never sent it, so she basically was neglected of an education." Eventually, because of all her school absences, a judge ordered Brittany's removal from her mother's home. Although her older sisters were still attending school, "when they take one, they take all," so all three of the daughters under age 18 were taken back into foster care. But Shelly was 19 at the time, so she was allowed to remain at home.

Only a few months later, Shelly, her older sister (who also had a child), and Beth were evicted from their apartment and were forced to return to the EAU. It was Shelly's first time appealing for shelter as an adult. However, she was so appalled by the conditions that she left the facility before filing any paperwork.

While pregnant with Anastasia, Shelly began spending

time with an old friend named Raheem. Aaron had all but disappeared when she became pregnant, and Raheem had stepped in and started looking out for Shelly during her pregnancy and after her daughter's birth. So when she and her family went to the EAU, Shelly called Raheem and he and his mother invited her and Anastasia to stay with them at their apartment.

Initially the relationship was good, and Raheem and his mother treated Shelly and her daughter well. Their friendship soon turned romantic and Raheem became a father figure to the baby. "Basically he was my daughter's father. He did everything. The baby cried, he got up, he fed her. He did the little things. And then I became pregnant, and that's when he did the bad things."

Anastasia was only six months old when Shelly became pregnant with her second child. Raheem was adamantly against having a child, but neither he nor Shelly could afford an abortion. The couple began to argue over the pregnancy and eventually they broke up. Yet Shelly had nowhere else to go with her young daughter, so she stayed in Raheem's home.

Shelly managed to find a hospital that would perform an abortion for free, but by then she was too far along in her pregnancy. "I finally had the oomph to try to get an abortion, but I was too far along for the hospital to do it. I'm just like . . . two children? I can't have two kids. I'm only 20. What am I going to do with two kids?" Adding to her stress was the fact that her disagreements with Raheem had escalated into physical abuse. "I'm trying to weigh my options. It was just so verbal, so physical; the grabbing, slamming me against the wall, backhand smacks."

One afternoon the couple got into an argument over

Shelly's public assistance check; she says that Raheem stole the money allotted to buy food for her daughter. His mother was home at the time, and the tension that had been building for months erupted into a physical fight. Shelly was seven months pregnant with her son, and she describes falling to the floor in the fetal position while Raheem and his mother kicked her in the face and abdomen. The fight only stopped when Raheem's brother-in-law came home and intervened. Shelly suffered a broken rib from the incident, and had to stay in the hospital for a week so that her baby could be monitored. By this point, she was so afraid of her boyfriend that at the hospital she lied to the doctor, telling him that she had fallen down the stairs.

Shortly after the fight, Shelly took her daughter to visit Aaron, who was serving time in jail. When Aaron saw her black eye, he was furious that she would put their daughter in an abusive situation and made her promise to leave. When she realized that her infant daughter was having nightmares because of the abuse she witnessed, Shelly knew that it was finally time to leave. "It was done in front of her. She was an infant and she was having nightmares. It was like, how many times are you going to cry yourself to sleep, Shelly? You just have to wake up and realize that you're [going to be] a single parent with two children." Faced with no alternative, and pregnant with her second child, Shelly brought Anastasia back to the Bronx homeless facility.

At the EAU

At the time, the EAU was trying to decrease the number of families entering the shelter system through a "diversion program," an alternative to the normal track. Instead of entering the system, the City would pay the necessary upfront costs for an apartment.[4] Shelly decided to participate in this program. With the help of a sympathetic real estate broker who could tell from her facial bruises that she was leaving an abusive relationship, Shelly found an apartment in Brooklyn, and the city covered the cost of the first month's rent, security deposit, and broker's fees.

Although it seemed like the best choice at the time, Shelly now describes going into the diversion program as "the easy road out." Nine months pregnant and caring for a year-old daughter, she just wanted to get out of the EAU as quickly as possible. "It was so crowded and nobody was attending to us. So it was like, they don't care. They have a home."

Now on public assistance, Shelly and her children were allotted a $286 monthly shelter allowance. The rent on her apartment was $550, leaving her contribution at $264. Although she was working, between the costs of babysitters, utilities, and food, she could hardly afford the monthly payment. Shelly struggled, barely getting by, for two years. In the third year, she fell behind in her rent.

Shelly also became involved in a new relationship with a man she doesn't like to discuss. The new boyfriend was not physically abusive, but he was emotionally abusive and unhappy with the idea of her making more money than him. On more than one occasion, Shelly found higher paying employment, only to be forced to quit by his physical threats.

---

4. The "Diversion Program" enabled homeless families without sufficient capital to rent their own apartments, effectively diverting some families from city shelters. Families in turn only needed to provide a third party to cosign their lease. The program no longer exists.

Help from Jiggetts

During the last year in her Brooklyn apartment, Shelly was relying on Jiggetts assistance to help pay her rent.[5] Although Jiggetts enabled her family to remain in their apartment, she describes it as "not worth it." To receive Jiggetts assistance, recipients have to be on welfare, and their rent must already have been in arrears, which frequently results in an eviction. Because of Jiggetts stipulations, Shelly was evicted repeatedly, "like every three months," she says. Usually these evictions would only last four or five days, and she would stay with a friend until the Jiggetts money came through and they were able to move back into the apartment.

Ironically, it was when her landlord decided to sell the building to the City of New York to build a homeless shelter that Shelly found herself back at the EAU. Well aware of how trying the experience had been for her and her sister, Shelly initially resisted returning there. She describes sitting down with her family to tell them, "I think, at this point, they're trying to buy my apartment and turn it into a shelter. I said, 'I'm going to try to find a new one. You know, as hard as I can I'm going to look. If I don't find anything,' I said, 'my last resort is definitely going to be the EAU.'"

Shelly's family had such an extended history with homelessness that for them, the shelter system was almost a right of passage, a necessary step towards becoming an adult. Her mother and sisters were familiar with the process, and they were able to give

---

5. A New York City program created as a result of a lawsuit claiming that shelter allowances do not fully cover the average cost of city apartments. Jiggetts relief paid the difference between a family's rent and their shelter allowance, in this case $264. The program was modified in May 2005 and is now called Family Eviction Prevention Supplement (FEPS).

Shelly guidance and advice. Shelly viewed entering the shelter system as a way to get her life back on track. "I sat down, I said, 'Mom, right now it's time for me to get myself together. I've got two children; I don't have no goals, no job, nothing. I'm not going to say I feel like a loser, but I have too much ambition for that.' And to top it off, I was in a bad relationship." Shelly left the man she had been dating and returned to the EAU in May 2002.

Another Try

Shelly repeatedly refers to the EAU as "the worst part of the experience." Her children were miserable and unable to sleep or eat while they were there. Shelly's son was particularly affected by the experience. "The whole time we were in EAU, he laid in my lap. He didn't move, he didn't play, he didn't touch anything. He just kept saying, 'It's dirty, it's dirty, it's dirty.' He kept asking me, 'Why Mommy? Why do you have me here?'"

The night of their arrival, they had to sleep on the facility's floor. The next night, at around three o'clock in the morning, they were placed in an overnight shelter only to be brought back to the EAU a few short hours later. Like all families applying for shelter, their next move was to a ten-day conditional placement while they awaited a decision on their eligibility for shelter.[6]

While it was only intended as a ten-day placement, and shelter regulations stipulate that stays in these temporary facilities

6. The application for shelter involves a 10-day assessment period during which families stay in a conditional placement. While applying for shelter at the Emergency Assistance Unit (EAU) or the Prevention Assistance and Temporary Housing (PATH) intake center families are required to provide the names and addresses of all residences from the two years preceding homelessness. Caseworkers then call or visit these residences to determine whether or not families may return there. Despite 10-day limits, assessment periods can, and often do, last for weeks.

must be limited to thirty days or less, Shelly and her children stayed at the conditional shelter for three months. "It was because the shelter system is overcrowded," Shelly says about this period, with a world-weariness atypical of a 26 year old.

Staying in Shelter

At the end of July 2002, Shelly and her children were transferred to a Tier II shelter in the Bronx.[7] There, she could begin her paperwork, apply for a Section 8 housing voucher and public housing, and attend classes and job-training programs.[8]

When she first arrived, however, Shelly says she couldn't stop crying. In part, she felt a profound sense of defeat, finally having found herself in a place she'd been trying so desperately to avoid. She was also upset about the lack of privacy and the fact that families had to share bathroom facilities. Shelly describes calling her mother and crying on the phone to her, but her mother, having been through the system herself, knew how it worked and encouraged Shelly to stay put. "My mother was like, 'Just hang in there.' She was like, 'You're a strong one.' I was like, I can't do this. My kids are not used to certain things, I did not want to put them through it. But my mother said, 'It's only temporary. Do what you have to do, and you'll be out of there in no time.' So, I did what I had to do. I joined classes."

Shelly describes her time at the family shelter in mostly positive terms. She and the other mothers on her floor got along

---

7. Tier II Shelters are nonprofit operated facilities for homeless families with children 18 or younger.
8. Section 8 is a federal housing subsidy for low-income renters that pays the difference between 30 percent of the renters' incomes and the fair market rent.

well and formed a network of support, watching each other's children and helping each other through the complicated housing application process.

She does express frustration with her former caseworker at the shelter. "My caseworker figured I was going to be somebody who was lazy and wasn't going to take on a challenge. The first day I got there and he was asking me all these questions about foster care and welfare and stuff. His exact words were, 'Damn! You had a bad life.' Ok, so you just automatically assume that I'm going to repeat what's been done? I just basically told him, 'Don't stereotype me.' But he realized he couldn't break me. He thought I wasn't going to be up for the challenge, but I was always up for the challenge."

Determined not to get "stuck," Shelly took advantage of her time at the shelter, and treated it as an opportunity for growth. She earned her GED,[9] participated in a job-training program, and attended classes to become a licensed day care provider, all the while keeping her focus on the greater goals of securing an apartment and a well-paying job. "I knew it was going to be a temporary situation, so I treated it like a temporary situation. I didn't let myself get comfortable. I did what I had to do. I never missed an appointment, and I worked and I just did what I had to do to get out of there."

Shelly also took a lot of pride in her room. She set it up as a sort of mini-apartment, complete with sofa (made from one of the beds) and dining table. She says, "You have to make yourself

---

9. The General Educational Development Test (GED) is a certification test of high-school level academic skill.

comfortable. Even though you don't want to be there, you don't have to leave your room looking any old kind of way."

With the help of a housing specialist, Shelly applied for both a Section 8 federal housing subsidy and low-income housing through the New York City Housing Authority (NYCHA).[10] She was accepted to both programs, and immediately began looking for apartments. It was an experience that would prove one of the most frustrating parts of being a homeless parent.

The health of Shelly's son, Amir, was another important issue. From the moment that Shelly took her children to the EAU, her son suffered severe emotional stress and began to stutter when he spoke. Eventually, the strain of being homeless, going through the EAU, and moving between shelters began to cause physical ailments. He "couldn't really cope with things," Shelly says. He was unable to keep food down and subsisted almost entirely on crackers and ginger ale. To try to address the problem, she began bringing her son to Raheem's house on the weekends so he could have a bath, a home-cooked meal, and some sense of stability.

Anastasia fared better. "She was very strong, very strong-minded." Shelly says. She thinks that her daughter has mentally blocked out the majority of the time the family was homeless. "She remembers the good parts. So I think that's a good thing. She doesn't remember the bad parts—that we were at the EAU, that it was dirty. She doesn't remember that."

With the help of the shelter's job-training program, in November 2002, Shelly got a job at the upscale department store

---

10. NYCHA is a city agency that provides affordable housing throughout the five boroughs of New York City. NYCHA administers the majority of the City's affordable housing stock, including the "housing projects."

Bloomingdale's. It was the beginning of her first positive stretch in some time. In December, she found a two-bedroom apartment in a public housing complex in Harlem, and on December 11 she moved her family out of the shelter.

Working and Saving

Shelly has very clear goals, and her plans for the future revolve around ensuring that her children are raised in a happy, healthy, and stable environment. "I focus on . . . stabilization as far as my kids go. Cause I don't want to move around. . . . This is why after I came out of the shelter, my main focus was to have a good job. So I could pay my own rent and I don't have to worry. . . . Even if it's a dead-end job, I'm going to just have to stick it out, because I don't want to have my children experience what I've experienced. I do feel that I do deserve better, and as long as I work at it, I'm going to get better."

Shelly's job at Bloomingdale's was seasonal and ended after two months. Fortunately, she had kept in contact with the shelter's job training program and was sent on another interview just a few weeks later. She was hired as an office assistant at a construction company and in early 2005, she celebrated her two-year anniversary with the company. By all accounts, her work ethic is unparalleled. "They tell me all the time how thankful they are to have a person like me, because I basically devote my life to my job. That's my income, you know, if I don't have that, I don't have anything."

When it comes to her personal finances, Shelly exhibits a wisdom and maturity that seem beyond her years. She views today's hard work as an investment in tomorrow, all part of giving her children a better life than she had. Shelly makes just above minimum wage at the construction firm, but she has still managed to save considerably for herself and her children. "You can't let obstacles get in the way. You have to think about the future. I said now my kids have their own life insurance. I've been saving up life insurance for them since they were born. Plus college since they've been born. Five or ten dollars here, put in the bank. It's not even about having a lot of money. I'll live basically in poverty until my kids are old enough. And then they can live the way they want to live. You know, I'll be in low-income [housing]. But I'll build."

Anastasia and Amir

While at the shelter, Shelly and her children participated in a literacy program where parents were encouraged to read with their children. After they moved into their own apartment, Shelly brought those lessons to their new home. Today, she monitors her children's schoolwork carefully and reads with them on a regular basis. "We do a lot of work at home. On the walk to school, we count to fifty. We count forward and backwards. Not just the teachers, parents must do their part as far as homework. Stay on top . . . cause my mother didn't stay on top with us for homework. No she didn't. I get home, soon as I get home, I'm like, 'Is that homework done?' If not, let's get it done."

Today Shelly's children are thriving. She is the picture of a proud parent when boasting about her daughter's academic success. When Anastasia finished kindergarten she won an award for being the only child who could read a whole book cover to cover. "You know, the teacher said it's very rare for you to see a young mother's child be this way," she says, beaming.

Amir is happy and healthy as well. He no longer suffers from the physical symptoms of his emotional stress, and has returned to the happy, outgoing little boy he was before the family became homeless. In the fall of 2004, he was placed in the accelerated kindergarten class at school.

Although Shelly has been involved in romantic relationships since her last period of homelessness, she maintains that she will never again put herself in a situation where she has to rely on a man. Instead, one of her primary goals is to always be able to provide for herself and her children.

Six Sisters, the Same Story

Although several of her sisters still live in the New York area, Shelly is so busy with work and night classes that she has little contact with them. When talking about her sisters, she vacillates between sympathy and frustration. She is particularly critical when it comes to some of the financial decisions her sisters have made.

Her eldest sister went through the homeless shelter system too and is now on public assistance, living in Brooklyn with her three children. "My older sister is basically following in the same footsteps as my mother. She has never worked a day in her life. She doesn't even know how to fill out a job application. She can tell you more about what someone's wearing than what's going on in [her children's] school. My sister is so busy worrying about her kids wearing Prada and Chloe—*on welfare!*—instead of trying to get a job to save up money for better things. I know her children deserve better."

Shelly's other older sister had a baby at fourteen, the youngest of any of the sisters in the family. She too went through the shelter system but has since improved her life dramatically; she currently lives in her own house in North Carolina and works as a corrections officer. However, Shelly still worries about her niece. "Her daughter has been left back about five times. What is going on that there's no focus as far as the children?"

Shelly's two younger sisters are living in North Carolina as well. One has a baby and is currently enrolled in college. But Brittany, the youngest, is in kinship care with Kathy, the aunt who Shelly called a "hypocrite." "Brittany is not doing so well; at this point she's mentally ill. She's violent; I think [it] is more or less because of her emotions, because of what she's been through. She lost her father at a young age and then, you know, my mother is always sick with something."

Everyday Struggle

Shelly's story is remarkable. She has successfully stabilized her family and, by all accounts, her children are thriving. Yet, by no means have things gotten any easier. Subsisting on a single salary is tough to begin with, and $7.85 an hour is barely a living wage, especially with two young children. "If the cost of living wasn't so much, people would be able to survive. It's hard to survive in New York. It's really hard."

Shelly is proud of her two-bedroom apartment in a Harlem project, but she expresses frustration with the stigma of living in a housing project and police behavior toward her and her neighbors. She admits that she is sometimes frightened to come home, and has had enough troubling run-ins with violence, both with the police and her neighbors, that she says, "when I'm coming home, I don't know, it's just when I get off that train, it's like, let's just hope nothing happened today." Shelly is particularly concerned for her children, and worries about them growing up in such an environment. She is close to tears when talking about an incident in which two young police officers pulled their guns on a young man who they thought was smoking marijuana when Shelly and her children were just a few steps away. As it turned out, what they had thought was a joint was actually a cigarette.

Another unfortunate event occurred this year. A few weeks into the fall semester, Shelly's babysitter was arrested for buying cocaine on school property while on her way to pick up Anastasia and Amir. Shelly was shocked: the sitter had been recommended by neighbors and there had been no indication that she was a drug user. "It feels like just when things are going well, something comes along to knock me back down." She was stressed, worried about leaving her children with another sitter, and had to take a few weeks off from community college. Luckily, she found an after-school program where her kids could spend the afternoons, and she was soon back in classes.

Looking Forward

Shelly is considering moving South to join her sisters and mother. She knows her money would go farther, she might even be able to afford a three-bedroom house, so Anastasia and Amir could have their own rooms. Anastasia is excelling in school, especially in reading and writing; Shelly thinks she might grow up to become a writer or reporter.

Shelly says of her volunteer work with the auxiliary police, "I always wanted to be a cop. I'm going to weigh my options as far as the law goes. I can still do two years of law school . . . be a police officer and go to school at the same time . . . I'm never going to be able to see my children! But it's all for the best. So that they can have a better life."

Due to the circumstances of Shelly's upbringing, she was unable to complete high school. After having children as a teenager, it wasn't until she entered the shelter system that she had the opportunity to resume her education. Once she entered a transitional housing facility, Shelly was able to put her two young children in day care and after-school programs and attend classes at the shelter's alternative high school. At the high school, Shelly successfully achieved high school equivalency, learned how to use computers, and was referred to the shelter's job training program, all while her children acquired their own skills in the facilities downstairs.

CHAPTER TWO

Belle

Escaping Violence and Dependence

I had a pretty good life, I just went astray. I just basically needed structure. That's where the shelters came in.

On the surface, Belle's story seems typical: her homelessness was precipitated by a violently abusive marriage and heroin addiction. But viewing it simplistically glosses over the uniqueness of her story. She grew up in a happy, stable home, and her parents' marriage is so solid that in 2004, they happily celebrated their fiftieth wedding anniversary. She was raised with all the trappings of a middle-class childhood, including horseback-riding camp, vacations abroad, and dedicated, supportive parents. Today, looking back on her life's experiences, Belle repeats what so many women who have been through similar experiences say, that self-sufficiency was the most important lesson she learned. Were it not for her dependencies, everything might have been different.

Growing Up

In comparison to many women who have gone through the New York City shelter system, Belle's childhood was idyllic.

Born and raised in the Northeast Bronx, she describes a happy childhood where she and her two siblings grew up in relative privilege. The family owned their own home, and were financially stable, with her father working as a carpenter and her mother as a nurse. "I had a pretty good life. We went on vacation every year. I've seen Spain, Portugal. I saw Jamaica. Every summer we would go to camp. We had archery lessons, horseback riding. So that was good," she nods. "Yeah, that was good."

Before starting college, Belle took a year off and worked as a cashier on the Upper West Side of Manhattan. "I was like, 'Oh! I have my own money, and my own little job. I don't have to ask my mom for much of anything.'" Throughout the year, her parents saved half the money she was earning so that when Belle started community college that fall, they were able to buy her a car. "That's how they teach us to be responsible." It's a lesson Belle uses today with her own sons, "My son works. I don't take half his money. I just give him a bill. I say, 'You can do the phone. This is your responsibility.'"

An Unexpected Pregnancy

Growing up, Belle's childhood sweetheart was a boy named Dennis. Dennis lived with his mother in a Queens housing project, but his aunt lived next door to Belle. They met when they were ten and in grammar school called each other "girlfriend and boyfriend." After Dennis got back from a stint in the U.S. Marines, he and Belle started dating seriously. At twenty years old and one year into college, Belle became pregnant with his child.

Although she protested, Belle's father insisted that she and

Dennis marry. "My father was the one who proposed to us. When he found out I was pregnant, he proposed to me and my children's father. He told us, we will be married in the next month or so. 'Let's get working on these plans quick.'" Twenty-one years old and four months pregnant, Belle and Dennis got married.

Despite her initial reluctance to marry, it was a happy period at first. "I was excited, the whole marriage thing, having a baby, whole new thing! It wasn't all I thought it would be though. Everything was good at first, but then my husband turned out to be a monster."

Belle and Dennis moved into an apartment in the Bronx. Soon after, Belle gave birth to her first child, a son they named Devon. She withdrew from her classes at the community college with the intention of returning. The first signs of trouble came when Belle re-enrolled in school after having her baby. Dennis became extremely jealous and grew intolerant of Belle's life outside their home. Sometimes a study group or homework would keep Belle out of the house until the evening, and she would come home to find Dennis extremely agitated, and occasionally even violent.

The Courage to Leave

Eventually Belle dropped out of school altogether. "I could have finished, but it was just too much aggravation and just too much violence. . . . It was easier to quit." It's a decision she still regrets. Dennis, who was working in construction, grew increasingly abusive throughout the marriage. Belle faults herself for not leaving him sooner, but maintains that she was too young and didn't have the strength to leave him. "When you get into a relationship like that, it's hard to get away . . . you get stripped of your self-esteem." Two years after giving birth to Devon, she gave birth to another son.

Belle thinks that Dennis's abuse might have had to do with her privileged childhood. He called her "uptown girl," and Belle suspects that he was jealous of her background. "I came from a background where my parents had a home, we went to plays, I ice-skated, we traveled, whereas he never did any of those things. His mother was a struggling single parent, and she lived in the projects." She pauses, "Coming up, he didn't have the things that I had, so I think that's where the problem came in at."

Since dropping out of college, Belle had been working at a group home for developmentally disabled adults. She enjoyed the job, but the facility moved to a location further from her home. Although the new group home was still located in the Bronx, Dennis' jealousy flared at the prospect of Belle traveling farther to work and spending more time away from him and the children. Belle subsequently quit her job. "He was just being a real jerk about it, so to me, it was just easier to make peace, and to do what he asked me to do."

Belle still regrets leaving the position, because it only increased her dependency on her abusive husband. "I let him be the breadwinner. And that's a big mistake, when you let a man tell you what to do. I know that now. That could never, ever happen again. But that's the kind of relationship I was in at the time. Being that it was my first relationship, my first marriage, I didn't know. I figured that's the way things go."

Periodically, Belle tried to leave Dennis, but it was never longer than a week or two before he convinced her to come back. "You know, you start to believe everything, 'Oh yeah, he'll change. He won't wake up and punch me in my jaw today.'" She was also hesitant to break up the family. "I wanted it to work. You try to keep the family together. And [anyway] at that time, they didn't have places you could go. I tried, and one [domestic violence shelter] told me I would have to wait two weeks, three weeks before I could go. By that time we was chummy again."

Belle knew that she would have to leave eventually, if not for her sake, then for her children's. Dennis was not physically abusive to the children, but Belle considers their having witnessed violence towards her a form of mental and emotional abuse. "[He was] abusive to them mentally because they saw their mom get beat up and the fighting and the cursing. That will take a toll on a child."

Belle had been married to Dennis for ten years before she finally summoned the courage to leave. She took her two sons, who were then ten and eight years old, and moved in with her parents. Dennis pursued and for a period even stalked them. "He was trying to get his family back," she explains.

But Belle stood her ground. "How did I leave? My [friend] came into town from Florida. And when he came in, I grew chutzpah. I grew balls." Belle's childhood friend, Maurice, was living in the home next door to Belle's parents. It was a relief for Belle. She knew that if Dennis came looking for her, or was threatening towards her, Maurice was right there to protect the family. "He was always a friend to me, so I knew that I could call him. So, I got brave." Finally, Dennis moved out of their apartment, and Belle and her children moved back in.

Maurice

Two years after separating from Dennis, Belle began dating Maurice. She was living with her two sons, working at the group home again, and making extra money working in flower shops. Eventually Maurice moved in with Belle and the boys. He owned his own construction company, and Belle quit her jobs to help him with his books. "Sometimes I even wore my [tool] belt and helped him on site."

Later, Belle found out that Maurice had earned the money to start his construction company by dealing drugs. He had started out selling marijuana but eventually began selling cocaine as well. While he was running the construction company, Maurice continued to deal drugs on the side. "I didn't know at first. After he moved in with me, then I found out. I thought he was just selling weed, not that it's any better, but it's not cocaine. But the cocaine then turned into crack, and then next thing I knew, stuff started escalating."

Maurice was also an active drug user and eventually started shooting heroin. "He was a strange character when he used. I remember being with my kids, we'd be like, 'No, we're not going in that house till he comes down off that shit.'"

Belle had no prior history of drug use, but the drugs were around her all the time, with dealers and users coming and going from their apartment. Before long, she started experimenting. "[Maurice] was like, 'Oh, just try some.' Me being weak-minded,

I tried it. I mean, it's like they say, you hang out at a barbershop, pretty soon you going to get a haircut. I got the haircut. And it'd been going downhill from that time until I came [to the shelter]."

Addiction

What started as experimentation quickly spun out of control, and soon Belle was using crack, cocaine, and heroin. "I took the heroin to come down off the coke. I took the crack to get up off the heroin. I was using everything. Something to bring you up, something to bring you down. That's how it went. A crazy roller coaster." Now, Belle looks back at the period when she was addicted to drugs and seems amazed that there was a time when she lived like she did. "I mean, I really don't know how I lived that way. . . I don't know how I survived."

Belle still had custody of her two sons while she was living with Maurice and growing dependent on drugs. Today she calls crack "the devil's drug," because not only do the users suffer, but their children suffer as well. Belle's situation was unique, however. Her parents were supportive and available, and frequently took care of the children. With their unwitting help, Belle managed to keep her sons neat, clean, and well-fed while she was using. "I will not take credit for that. It was due to my mom and dad. They were like my enablers."

Maurice and Belle had been living together for nearly five years when Belle became pregnant again; it was her third pregnancy and she was actively using drugs. Belle went to her doctor and told him that she had been using heroin, figuring that he would find out anyway. Initially, she wanted to quit the heroin cold turkey, but her doctor convinced her that it would be more damaging to the baby than using, so he persuaded her to go on methadone instead. "She came out toxic anyway," Belle says. Her new baby, Larisse, spent the first two weeks of her life in the hospital, detoxifying from the methadone.

Although methadone enabled Belle to keep Larisse, she is critical of the drug and of methadone programs in general. She laughs when recounting how the clinic sent a free bus to bring her and other addicts to the hospital to pick up their drugs. "Isn't that crazy? Every morning." Mainly, Belle is critical of programs that replace one addiction with another, legal, addiction. "That's another devil's drug. A legal devil's drug. And that's crazy—that's just switch-hitting."

For the next two years, Belle sporadically participated in methadone programs and was in and out of outpatient treatment programs. One morning she left her three children with a neighbor so that she could go pick up her methadone at the clinic and while she was out, her ex-husband Dennis stopped by to see the boys. The neighbor knew Dennis, since he had once lived in the building too, so she let him take the boys with him. Later that day Belle went to his house to pick them up, but, aware of her drug use, Dennis refused to let them go. Belle and Dennis hadn't worked out a formal agreement over the custody of their children. Without any paperwork, there was nothing Belle or the police could do to get them back.

Belle was forced to go to court to legally petition for sole custody. For the duration of the four-month custody dispute, the children were not allowed to stay with either Belle or Dennis and stayed with Dennis's mother instead. Ultimately, Belle won sole custody of both children, with the stipulation that she attend methadone programs regularly and get real help with her addiction.

Even though Belle was picking up her methadone and being monitored through urine samples, she continued to use drugs. "An addict will do what an addict has to do. I used other people's urine, but I was still using." Maurice also continued to actively use and sell drugs.

When Larisse was a year old, Belle's parents decided to move to South Carolina, taking Larisse with them. Without her enablers, Belle spiraled downwards. She knew that the situation was dire and that she needed help. Anticipating checking herself into a rehabilitation program, Belle sent her sons to live with their father, who had since remarried. "I kind of sent my sons away before I went into the shelter because I didn't want them to see me the way I was." After sending her sons to their father's house, Belle found herself "a free agent," with all three of her children living with relatives. She stalled for several months before finally seeking help.

Trying to Leave

Finally, Belle realized that the first step to getting treatment would be leaving the home she shared with Maurice. She left the apartment and checked herself into an inpatient drug treatment program. "When I left, I just walked away with the clothes on my back. I left everything there and I never returned." However, soon after she arrived at the treatment program, she found out that she was pregnant again. The facility didn't allow pregnant women or children, so Belle had to leave. Her parents were still unaware of her drug addiction, so she didn't feel that she could turn to them for help. Instead, she decided to go to the Emergency Assistance Unit (EAU).[1]

Belle stayed at the EAU for three days. "It's not somewhere that you would really want to be, but you make the best of a bad situation, with expectations that the next step would be better." From there, she was taken to an assessment facility in the Bronx.[2]

While Belle was there, her parents brought Larisse up to stay with her. However, the conditions at the facility were so sub-standard that Belle's daughter became severely ill and had to be hospitalized. "My oldest daughter would not eat in there. In fact, she had to be hospitalized for dehydration because she would not eat or drink. That's how bad the conditions were. In the hospital, they asked me what happened [to Larisse], so I had to explain to them about this place."

Belle was now nine months pregnant with her fourth child. Knowing that she was about to give birth again, and that her young daughter was already sick, concerned hospital staff called the Department of Health. "Next thing I know, they were shipping me out of there." Concerned about her health, Belle's parents again took Larisse down to South Carolina.

Belle was subsequently taken to a transitional shelter in the

---

1. The Emergency Assistance Unit is the gateway to the City shelter system.

2. The application for shelter involves a 10-day assessment period during which families stay in a conditional placement. While applying for shelter at the Emergency Assistance Unit (EAU) or the Prevention Assistance and Temporary Housing (PATH) intake center families are required to provide the names and addresses of all residences from the two years preceding homelessness. Caseworkers then call or visit these residences to determine whether or not families may return there. Despite 10-day limits, assessment periods can, and often do, last for weeks.

Bronx, where she stayed until she gave birth to her fourth child, a daughter she named Elise. She still hadn't received proper attention for her substance abuse issues, and was still on methadone. After giving birth to Elise, her case manager suggested she move to a shelter in Queens that had an on-site drug rehabilitation program, one of few such programs that would allow her to bring her children along. "At that time, it was the help I needed, and I was able to bring my children."

Detox

The Queens shelter was like the one in the Bronx in that it was classified as transitional housing for families. However, this shelter had a multitude of programs available that were essential to Belle's recovery. First and foremost, they had two floors dedicated to women with substance abuse problems. Belle was able to keep her newborn baby with her while she went through detoxification and recovery.

Detoxifying from the methadone proved the hardest part of the entire experience. "Methadone was the hardest thing to ever kick. I had to get help and get off this stuff. It took me twenty-eight days to detox. And that means no sleep. It's rough. That's something I wouldn't wish on my enemy." Belle remembers being too weak to hold her own baby.

She recalls the shelter staff as helpful, encouraging her and ultimately helping her take the steps necessary to get off drugs. "I mean the staff is really good. They're really concerned. You know some people just work; they're just there because it's a job. These people, as far as I'm concerned, were genuinely, you know, they were concerned. And when I messed up, they put their foot in my ass. 'Get your act together. No more pity parties. Get up and do what you have to do for yourself.' And, you know, it worked."

As part of her treatment, Belle had to tell her parents about her drug addiction. Up until this point, they had thought that Belle was only in the shelter because she wanted to get away from Maurice. After all the support her parents had given her over the years, Belle found it extremely difficult to be honest about her problem. "It was just that, I didn't want to admit it. That's not something you want to tell your parents—'Yeah, Mom, I'm a junkie.' That's not something you want to admit to. That was the hardest thing I ever had to do. But I did it."

Her parents brought Larisse up with them, so at this point Belle had both of her daughters in the shelter with her, which proved helpful to her recovery. "My babies attended the day cares there, and I got really involved with the day care. I mean . . . at one time I was in a slump, because I was like, ah, I'm in a shelter, but they had a lot of programs to offer. But, [it was good] to get involved with the children, because you know, children uplift you. I was the mother that was always in daycare, bringing food, chocolate for their milk."

Aside from helping out in the daycare center, Belle also joined a program aimed at improving parent and child literacy and encouraging families to read together. She already had her high school diploma and had attended a few years of college, but she describes joining the program as an emotionally proactive move. "Actually it was just doing something with my time while I was here. You know, doing something positive. You don't sit in the room and watch soap operas all day. That's something you don't do. You do something so you don't get depressed."

Belle was determined to get out of the shelter as quickly as possible, and she was successful, moving out one day short of a year. "You know there are some women where, when they get in the system, they get stuck in the system. I was not going to be one of those women. I had to get out."

With the help of the shelter's housing specialist, Belle applied for and received a Section 8 housing voucher and moved from Queens to a small house in Far Rockaway, Brooklyn.[3] She lived there with her children for two years, until the house was sold. "I was running around like a chicken with her head cut off trying to find housing cause I didn't want to end up back in the shelter. But I found it. I guess if you do your footwork, you'll get what you need." Fortunately, Belle was able to find an apartment in Queens, only fifteen minutes away from the shelter where she now works.

For Belle, the most important part of the experience was the restoration of her self-esteem. "When I lived [in the shelter], they helped me get charge of my life and realize nobody should tell me what to do. I do what I feel and know in my heart is right. They gave me back my self-esteem. No man could ever walk in my life today and tell me what to do. No man, no woman."

Today

Shortly after leaving the shelter, Belle was hired by its

---

3. Section 8 is a federal housing subsidy for low-income renters that pays the difference between 30 percent of the renters' incomes and the fair market rent.

recreation department and has been working there ever since. "I enjoy my job here, the people I've met. You know, it's like, I don't know any other way to put it but ever since I came here, my whole life has changed. And it's changed for the better. You know, it's a positive move. Not all shelters . . . you know, this shelter offers a lot. For people who don't have their high school diploma, they have the [literacy] program.

"One thing I like about my job is the gratification from the children. There's times, like when they come off the bus from [the shelter's summer] camp, they're like, 'Miss Belle!' grab me and hug me. Like when I go up to camp, I'm guaranteed at least ten hugs. And that makes you feel good. I know it makes me feel good."

Belle loves her position at the facility; she truly enjoys working with the children and helping to make their lives better. To try to make up for shortcomings she perceives on the part of the parents, she and the recreation staff are very attentive to the children's needs. "They respect us and they'll listen to what we have to say. If we see them not going to school, we jump on them and then we start checking them to make sure they're going to school. We want to see report cards. I mean, we really get involved in these children's lives."

Part of Belle's job involves traveling to other homeless shelters to pick up children and bring them to the summer camps her employer runs, so she has become an expert on the various facilities. "I go to some of the other shelters, they don't have GED programs, they don't have computer classes.[4] You go in their recreation

4. The General Educational Development Test (GED) is a certification test of high-school level academic skill.

department, it may be [tiny], look how big ours is. And we have the library over there. You got about fifteen computers over there. And the kids take advantage of it. It's not just for show, the kids can use it. So, firstly you don't get in here and get comfortable. Utilize the programs and get the hell out. Get out and do what you have to do."

At this point, Belle has met and worked with hundreds of homeless mothers. She's seen women like herself, who were able to move through the system relatively quickly, and women who seem to get stuck, languishing in the shelters, unable to move forward. "You have a lot of people. . . . They just get stuck. But you got to do what you got to do. You don't just sit here and let the system beat you. You got to beat it."

Looking Forward

At the moment, Belle is living with her younger son, who is twenty-two, and her two daughters, who are ten and twelve years old. Her three-bedroom apartment is just big enough for the family, but Belle's father has offered to help with a down payment so she's hoping to buy a co-op or condo of her own. For now, she wants to stay in Queens. "I don't go to the Bronx because of all the things that happened to me in the Bronx. It's easier for me just to stay in Queens. I'm happy. I'm content."

Belle is very close with her parents, and frequently visits them in South Carolina. "My dad just loves me to death. And my mom loves me to death, too. Because I'm still doing what I have to do for me and mine."

She is also close with her children, and is particularly

proud of her sons and her relationship with them. "I mean like now, I could look in my son's eyes and you know, I see the difference, like 'Yeah, that's my mom!' Not, 'Oh God, that's my mother.' That's something I wouldn't trade for anything."

Belle's home is emphatically drug and violence free. "You cannot raise your voice or your hand in my household. That's just the way it is. I mean, after going through it, being subjected to it for so long . . . that's not a way to live. That's not a way for anyone to live. Now my son is so big, he wouldn't let a man come in there and touch me anyway. I got my sons on my side, I got God on my side, and I got Bolo, my dog, on my side. I got a lot going on."

Belle was able to finally seek help for her drug addiction because she found a facility that would accommodate her rehabilitation while she maintained custody of her infant daughter. Today, many transitional housing facilities offer such arrangements, as well as crisis nurseries that can care for a child without threat to custody while a parent recovers from addiction, domestic violence, or other personal issues that may prevent her from caring for the child in the way that she would like. The basic assurance that a child will be safe and protected while a parent receives the help that she needs often proves pivotal for parents who need assistance.

CHAPTER THREE
Angela

Bouncing Back from Financial Ruin

You know what, being strong about it helped me. But if I had to do it again, I don't think I would. I really don't. I think I would just leave New York altogether.

The events of September 11, 2001, had a devastating effect on the lives of nearly every New Yorker, from the richest to the poorest. The financial ramifications were tremendous, and shortly after the tragedy, the City's shelter system swelled. Angela and her children represent one of these stories.

Smart, soft-spoken, and warm, it's easy to see why Angela has been so successful in her career as a customer service representative for major national banks. She has been working in finance for nearly two decades, and currently is the go-between for investors and representatives, placing annuity trades and mutual fund trades for her customers. For her, homelessness was a brief, singular experience, directly related to the events of September 11, 2001, and brought about solely by financial difficulties. Hers is a story that speaks across racial, financial, and socio-economic backgrounds, proving that homelessness can happen to anyone and is

41

sometimes precipitated by just a few unlucky events that happen to coincide.

Family Relationships

Angela grew up in New York City, the child of generations of hard-working women. She was an only child until she was thirteen, but her mother was determined not to spoil her. "She taught me, you're an only child but you can't be spoiled. You've still got to be independent." When Angela's younger brother was born, the thirteen-year age difference meant that Angela was almost like a parent to him. The two are still close, and he treats Angela almost as if she were his mother. "He's still a big baby. He gets sick, and he cries for me."

In discussing her current success and strength, Angela credits her mother and grandmother with setting positive examples for her to follow. Today, Angela works nearly twelve-hour days, still manages to have home-cooked meals for her three children every night, and is involved in their school and homework. She credits her ability to work so hard for herself and her children to the positive example set by her family. "If you're used to it, or if you're accustomed to it, if you grow up in that type of family, it goes a long way. Cause my mom was the same way, my grandmother was the same way."

Starting a Family

Angela met the man who would be the father of her children in 1988. It was right after high school and Angela had taken a job at the Federal Reserve Bank, where Jeffrey worked as well.

The story has become a family legend, and their three children ask to hear it over and over again. According to Jeffrey, Angela wouldn't pay him any attention, even though he had a crush on her. "He tells the kids that story all the time, 'Your mother was really a snob, but then after I almost fell and busted my butt, then she wanted to talk to me.' I was like, 'Oh please, why you want to tell them that story? That's not true.' But it's true, it's true."

A year after they met, Angela gave birth to her first child, a daughter they named Jasmine. Three years later, their son Kevin was born. Their youngest son, Kareem, is just five years old. Although Jeffrey and Angela were never formally married, they lived together as man and wife for many years, and they shared responsibility for their three children. Their relationship had its rocky periods, however, and the two were separated at times.

One point of contention between Angela and Jeffrey involved his family. Jeffrey's mother never approved of their relationship and was vocal in her criticism of Angela. Her primary criticism stemmed from the fact that Angela had her children out of wedlock, but she was also critical of Angela's independence.

During their periods of separation, Angela did not ask Jeffrey for money or support, preferring to care for the children and herself independently. His mother perceived this as aloofness and thought that Angela was a snob. "I guess her kids grew up where they had to depend on someone. They always depended on a man. . . . If I've got to go somewhere, I'll take public transportation, I'll get in a cab. I'll go. I'm not sitting around calling for someone to come pick me up. [And] I'm not going to call and track you down and say 'Look, I need money for this, I need money for that.' I never called him for nothing. So they felt that, 'Oh well, she thinks she's too good.'"

The longest period of separation came when Jeffrey was laid off from his job. The couple had been together for ten years, and Angela thinks that Jeffrey panicked. Without a steady income, he was afraid he wouldn't be able to provide for the family and was probably a little threatened by Angela's independence and success at work. Ultimately, Jeffrey decided to move to Charleston, South Carolina, where he had family. "He was like, 'I can't make it in New York. It's hard to find a job.' I was like, 'Okay, but you can't just leave.' And then he just up and left, and there was a whole big fallout." Angela was furious at him for leaving her and the children when times got tough. In particular, she wanted her sons to have a father figure in their lives. But Angela relied on her independence and had her own successful career to fall back on—she was confident that she could support the family and keep them together on her own.

September 11, 2001

Angela steadily worked her way up the career ladder, finally landing a fairly lucrative position at a large, multinational investment advising firm. In the fall of 2001, she had been working there for eleven years. However, the events of September 11, 2001, and the ensuing economic slump were particularly devastating to finance and investment firms, many of which went out of business or enacted sweeping lay-offs. Following September 11, Angela's firm immediately started downsizing. Between the fall of 2001 and 2004, her office went from employing more than 300 people to fewer than ten. During the downsizing, Angela was laid off.

Initially, she didn't panic. She had been smart with her income, had managed to save a percentage of her salary, and was eligible for unemployment. She immediately set about collecting her unemployment benefits and looking for a new job. She also took advantage of her new schedule by volunteering at her children's schools, spending two days a week at each. "I was always involved, and that I enjoyed, because it gave me time to [be with the kids]. Usually when I had them, I went straight back to work. So, it gave me a time to be with them."

As time went by and the market failed to recover, Angela was unable to find a new position. "I collected unemployment, but it still wasn't enough to cover the full rent." She started to dip into her savings. "Little bit here, little bit there, with the rent and utilities and everything." Eventually, Angela had no choice but to give up the apartment in Queens and move in with her aunt in Brooklyn.

Doubled-Up

Although Angela's aunt welcomed her and the children, the apartment only had one bedroom and was too small for two women and three children. Angela took her children from Brooklyn to their schools in Queens every morning and spent the afternoons looking for a new apartment and a job. The conditions in her aunt's apartment quickly grew unbearable. It was overcrowded, but the situation only worsened once Angela's unemployment benefits ran out, and she was no longer able to contribute to rent or expenses.

Angela looked frantically for a new apartment, but every place she saw required two months rent up front, which by that point she couldn't afford. "One month's rent, a month's security. Trying to pay that, and I already took money out of my investment plan to try to maneuver, to make sure [the kids are] well taken care of, and I'm taken care of. I didn't have any more. I exhausted everything." However, it was clear that it was time for her and the kids to leave her aunt's apartment. "It was just her, and then the four of us, and we made it for so long and then when unemployment stopped, I was like, ok, now what am I going to do? We can't stay here because we really don't have enough space. So that winter, that's when the Salvation Army came to the house and picked us up."

Angela was completely unfamiliar with homeless services in New York City and was unaware of New York's Right to Shelter guarantee,[1] but the local Salvation Army would periodically go through her aunt's Brooklyn neighborhood and drop off flyers offering services to families at risk of homelessness. Angela went into their offices and signed up for housing assistance. Unfortunately, they told her it would be a long process, and by this point, she and the children were desperate to leave her aunt's apartment. They had been there for a full year, and the two older children were practically teenagers. The situation was untenable.

At the Salvation Army's recommendation, Angela and her

---

1. In 1979, the Legal Aid Society began advocating on behalf of homeless singles and families. These lawsuits and subsequent court battles ultimately established the City's right to shelter laws. A mandate unique among urban areas, the laws legally require the City to provide shelter for those who can prove that they are homeless.

children entered the City's family homelessness system. A caseworker came to her aunt's house, they filled out some paperwork stating how many bags they would be bringing, and a van was sent to pick them up and drive them to the City's Emergency Assistance Unit (EAU).[2]

Entering the Shelter System

Angela had no idea what to expect from the EAU. The people from the Salvation Army tried to prepare her for the experience, but they glossed over the details and misled her about how long the process would take. "They said, 'You'll be here but within a couple of hours they're going to move you somewhere else.' But it wasn't that fast. It wasn't a couple of hours."

Like many women, Angela found the time at the EAU to be the worst part of the entire homelessness experience. "The EAU was terrible. [It] was horrible. . . . People were laying on top of the chairs and the benches and the floor and stuff." Angela was also troubled by the metal detectors and the fact that she had to take her belongings with her everywhere, fearing that if she left any of her bags for even a few minutes they might be stolen. For the two and a half days that they were at the EAU, she was unable to bring her children to school because they all needed to be present at the facility and examined by the nurse before being allowed into the system.

Angela says that the worst part of the EAU was feeling degraded by the staff. She was offended by their assumption that her children had different fathers and felt like their questions were

2. The Emergency Assistance Unit is the gateway to the City shelter system.

invasive and belittling. "He's telling you, 'Why you can't stay with this family member? Why you can't stay with that family member? Are you looking for a job? Why haven't you found a job?' They ask you questions like that to try to discourage you, to get you to say, 'Okay, you know what? I'll just go.' After you go through it, then you realize, there's a lot of homeless people that are like, 'These people degrade me. That's why I don't want to even go through that.'" Angela says that after her experience at the EAU, if she had to do it again she would rather leave New York than go through the system.

A Long Wait

Angela was assigned to a temporary shelter during her ten-day assessment period.[3] Like so many other women, what was supposed to be a short ten-day stay turned into weeks, and then months. Angela and her children were in a conditional shelter in the Bronx for a total of two and a half months, during which time she continued to take her children to school in Queens each day.

Fortunately, she was assigned a particularly helpful caseworker at the facility. Aware of the family's long daily commute from the Bronx to Queens, the caseworker managed to place the family in a larger, more comprehensive shelter in Queens, significantly closer to the children's schools.

---

3. The application for shelter involves a 10-day assessment period during which families stay in a conditional placement. While applying for shelter at the Emergency Assistance Unit (EAU) or the Prevention Assistance and Temporary Housing (PATH) office families are required to provide the names and addresses of all residences from the two years preceding homelessness. Caseworkers then call or visit these residences to determine whether or not families may return there.

New Opportunities

The new facility afforded Angela new opportunities. Eliminating the hours of commuting each day allowed her much more time to look for another job and to begin looking into housing options.

She immediately visited the shelter's job training program. "I met [the director]. I went to [the employment placement center]. She was like, 'I'm going to help you.' And it worked out good." The program director invited her to open houses sponsored by the shelter and sent her to a staffing agency that provided temporary and permanent employees to various companies in the city. Because of her extensive and impressive employment history, Angela was given temporary work almost immediately.

Assigned to a position much like the one she held at her previous job, she was hired as a temporary employee in mid-July. The following February, the firm hired her as permanent staff.

The new shelter also provided Angela with new opportunities for housing assistance. Her housing specialist immediately began helping her with applications for both Section 8 federal housing subsidies and New York City Housing Authority (NYCHA) apartments.[4] As soon as she was certified for Section 8, Angela began looking at apartments. "I was determined to get out of there. Once I became certified, I was looking, I was calling, I was gone." Angela quickly found an apartment in Queens, big enough for the family of four and close to the children's schools.

---

4. Section 8 is a federal housing subsidy for low-income renters that pays the difference between 30 percent of the renters' incomes and the fair market rent. NYCHA is an agency that provides affordable housing throughout the five boroughs of New York City. NYCHA administers the majority of the City's affordable housing stock, including the "housing projects."

She was afraid that being in the shelter would be hard on her children and that their schoolwork might suffer as a result. Fortunately, they did well, participating in the shelter's after-school program for teenagers and playing with other children in the recreation program. "It was hard. I could see that it was hard, but they were trying to be strong for me so I wouldn't see that it was hard on them. They did their work, their grades were still up. That's what I was scared of, that their grades would go down. But they kept their grades up."

By the middle of July, Angela had found work and a new apartment. The family moved out of the shelter, just six months after their arrival.

Back on Track

Angela continues to be a diligent worker. At the time of these interviews, she was working at a bank's offices on Long Island. She likes her job and enjoys interacting with clients. "I have customers that will not speak to anyone else but me," she says proudly. Since she's a customer service representative, she often has to deal with irate clients, but with her gentle nature, she's very successful. "Once you help them and they know you sympathize with them, they're willing to go all the way with you."

Although she enjoys her job, Angela has to commute an hour and a half each way, taking three different buses to get from the apartment in Queens to Long Island. It leaves her little time with her children, but she tries to compensate on the weekends. "Fridays, Saturdays, and Sundays is usually family time for us. I try to keep it that way. Because, you know, during the week, it's hustle and bustle, especially when they're in school. Cause when I come home, I'm checking homework, [there's] not really time to talk. I'm checking homework, warming up food, and by the time we're done with that, it's bedtime."

On Sundays, Angela cooks, preparing dinners for the following week. Every Friday, she takes the children out somewhere. Despite the long days, she still manages to volunteer her time to cook and help out with events at her children's schools, believing that parental participation is important. Often, Angela finds that she is the only parent who is contributing, so she volunteers to make extra food so that the children can have events like bake sales. Still, Angela confesses that she often feels guilty that she's unable to attend school events because of her obligations at work.

Jeffrey has moved back to New York City and is trying to make up for lost time. "We're trying now to smooth things out. I'm like, 'You have three kids. You've got to be a father to the boys. There has to be a man figure.'" They are trying to work things out, particularly for the sake of the children and the family, but it's difficult because of their history. "I was like, 'After we had the three kids and we had the problems and you went your way and I went mine, and then me going through this situation, it's hard, because you weren't there to help me. You weren't there for me.'" Despite her concerns, Angela truly wants to work things out with Jeffrey. In 2004, the couple got engaged.

In late 2004, Angela was laid off for a second time when her employer was taken over by a larger bank. Fortunately, this time her unemployment was brief. She had saved enough to sustain the family through the period when she was not working and obtained another position relatively quickly.

Looking Back, Looking Forward

Angela looks back on her experience as a homeless mother with mixed emotions. On the one hand, she says that if she had to do it over again, she wouldn't. At the time she was afraid that leaving New York and uprooting the children would be too difficult for them, but now she thinks it would have been a better alternative to homelessness. Unlike many of the people profiled in this book, Angela was entirely unfamiliar with shelters and homelessness before her own experience. A white-collar employee, she had been accustomed to a certain standard of living and was devastated to lose everything, especially in light of all her hard work. "I've always really pushed. So this was really hard for me. It was really hard."

At the same time, Angela views it as a learning experience, and sometimes she looks back on it as an ultimately positive period. "Everything was good. I'm glad I got out of it. It was an experience, but you learn from it. You learn from it. Like trying to be more well-situated. Space out some more money cause you never know what's going to happen."

Angela's extensive work history helped her to connect quickly with the shelter's job-training coordinator, who immediately sent her to job fairs and interviews. The shelter staff, with their extensive connections, were able to assist Angela more readily than would have been possible through more traditional routes, thereby expediting her move from dependence to self-sufficiency.

CHAPTER FOUR

Andre

One Father's Journey from Dealer to Youth Worker

My past is my past... I'm just blessed I've had a chance to feel like I'm making it up. I'm giving something back. That's how I look at it. I'm giving it back. I'm giving it back.

Sitting hunched over his workspace, with textbooks and notes piled up around him, it's difficult to imagine that this hard-working young college student has a criminal record and a history of homelessness. Although never a drug user, in his late teens and twenties Andre was involved in dealing crack cocaine. Like an astonishing percentage of young African-American men, he spent years in the criminal justice system, was branded early as a 'drug dealer,' and was never able to shake the stigma and blame that accompanies such a label.[1] Andre's story is an example of how people can get caught up in the legal system and, through a combination of events, never get out.

---

1. In 1995, one in three black men nationwide lived under some form of correctional supervision or control (prison, jail, parole, or probation). M. Maurer & T. Hurling, *Young Black Americans and the Criminal Justice System: Five Years Later.* (Washington DC: The Sentencing Project, 1995). In addition, an estimated 28.5 percent of black men will be admitted to prison during their lifetimes. Thomas Bonczar & Allen J. Beck, Ph.D. *Bureau of Justice Statistics Special Report: Lifetime Likelihood of Going to State or Federal Prison.* (Washington DC: U.S. Department of Justice, Office of Justice Programs, 1997).

To this day, Andre feels tremendous regret and anxiety over his past involvement with drugs. He is also one of the few men who entered the shelter system along with his partner and their children. In 2001, following Andre's third and final arrest, he, his longtime girlfriend Monica, and their three young children entered the New York City shelter system.

Childhood in Queens

Andre grew up in Queens, New York, the youngest child of a single mother who worked as a nursing assistant. His father was in the Army, stationed in Germany when Andre was a child. Andre's mother had two children by different men, and his father had what Andre describes as "a lot" of children. Andre's half-siblings were all significantly older, and many lived outside the city, so he had little contact with them. Because Andre's father was in the military, he was constantly traveling and being assigned to different posts around the world. Consequently, during Andre's early years, his mother was the only consistent family member. She doted on Andre, and the two had a close relationship.

Life in their small apartment in Queens was challenging. "It was kind of hard, but it was okay," he says about the period. His mother struggled to provide for Andre, hoping that he would never have to go without something he wanted. "My mother, she wasn't the richest person in the world, but whenever I needed anything I got it . . . and then some."

Things started to change when Andre was in his early teenage years. First, his mother met a man and soon became engaged. Andre was thirteen years old, and adjusting to having a new man in the house proved difficult. During the same period, Andre's father was transferred from Germany to Indiana. Although he hardly knew his father, and had never lived with him, the family collectively decided that Andre should join him in Indiana.

A New Home, A New Family

At the time, Andre's move to Indiana seemed to make a lot of sense. There was tension between him and his new stepfather, he had yet to have the opportunity to really get to know his father, and the schools and opportunities in Indiana seemed much more promising than his options in Queens. Plus, Andre showed great potential as an athlete and his father promised him that in Indiana the school sports programs were better, with experienced coaches and plenty of funding. If he excelled, Andre might even be able to secure a college scholarship.

Another factor that pushed Andre to move to Indiana was the fact that drugs, specifically crack cocaine, had started to make an appearance in his life in Queens. He was only in junior high, but already some of his classmates were starting to deal crack. "Oh man. It was the thing to do. I can remember being in the seventh grade having a friend that started selling it. Seventh grade . . . and he used to come to school with a whole lot of money all the time. And, you know, being young, you want to have the newest sneakers . . . back then I think Michael Jordans just came out, and you wanted to have those Jordans, you know what I mean?" Between the drugs and the promise of better opportunities, the move to Indiana seemed like a clear choice.

In Indiana, Andre's father had started another family, with

a new wife and three young children. Andre had not lived with siblings before, but he got along well with the younger kids and relished his role as big brother. The relationship between him and his stepmother was more difficult, however, and the two of them frequently clashed. Still, Andre liked Indiana, and particularly enjoyed living in a less urban area. "It was like an isolated community. Man, it was different. And, to be honest with you, if I had my way, I probably would try to raise my kids in that kind of community. It was like an [apartment] complex, but everybody knew everybody. Everybody's kids played with everybody."

Andre also felt that Indiana was less racially segregated than his neighborhood in New York, and his friendships with people outside his race had a significant impact on his perception of race relations. "When I was down there all my friends was white. I just started to see things in a different light when I got back. Like, you hear black people saying that like, 'The white man don't give you nothing.' It was real racial back when I was coming up. And you know, I went down there, and I seen that the people in New York don't know what they was talking about. That should have woke me up, but it didn't."

Andre stayed in Indiana for three years. He excelled in football and loved his suburban neighborhood, but tensions in the house were rising. His relationship with his father had started out strong, but it was becoming strained, in part because of the difficult relationship between Andre and his stepmother, with whom he continuously argued.

Andre hardly saw his mother, who remained in Queens with her husband. While he was in Indiana, Andre was active in sports, and she was working full time, so time and money for visits was scarce. "I think she missed me a lot and she just didn't want to say it." When he was seventeen, Andre decided to return to New York.

Andre remains conflicted about his time in Indiana. Sometimes he seems to regret ever going, saying, "It wasn't a good idea for me to go down there in the beginning." But Andre also seems to look at it as a positive experience of which he could have taken better advantage. "I wish I would have stayed down there sometimes. Coming back to New York just wasn't a good move for me, it just wasn't. I had more opportunities down there than I could ever imagine . . . in playing football. If you go to a high school, and you play football down there, that's like Football Town, USA. So, every single game you play you have scouts there from major colleges. I had a couple of people come to my house and talk to my father about me, but . . . after that, once I came to New York, I lost interest in sports." Andre says that had he stayed in Indiana, he "absolutely" would have received a scholarship to college.

Back to New York

When he got back to New York, Andre quickly resumed his friendships with kids he knew from school and the neighborhood. In Indiana, drugs and alcohol had been available, but nowhere near as prevalent as they were in Queens. Andre admits to "experimenting" but maintains that he simply didn't enjoy the effect alcohol and other substances had on him. "I experimented a couple of times, but I didn't like the way it made you feel. The most I ever did was like drink a beer or two. I would have drunk something socially, you know . . . just being social. [But] today, nah . . . it don't interest me. I think it's a waste of money, basically. I mean, if you do have something to drink, you might feel ok for a little bit, but you might have to spend twenty or thirty dollars just to feel okay. Nah, don't need it, don't need it."

Andre also consciously avoided substances after witnessing his mother's addiction to cigarettes. "Never smoked, never did nothing—because my mother smoked, she smoked cigarettes. And she had asthma, and I'd been seeing, she can't put them cigarettes down. She'd be having an asthma attack and still smoking the cigarettes. And I was like, 'I don't never want to go through nothing like that.'"

Andre can't remember any specific positive role models he had as a child or teenager. His understanding of addiction and aversion to substances comes instead from witnessing the negative impact substances had on those around him. "I had an uncle that used to drink a lot. He died a couple of years ago. But that's what killed him. Nobody could tell you why he drank, he couldn't tell you why he drank. That's what he liked to do. He used to spend every waking moment [drinking]. That right there told me alcohol ain't good for you. I seen a couple people I know, maybe a couple of years ago, the same age, that got involved in using drugs. That right there just made you just turn it off."

During this period of his life, Andre was spending most of his time with his friends, and many of them liked to drink alcohol and occasionally smoke marijuana. But while Andre attended their parties, he rarely drank or smoked, instead preferring to exercise or read. "I went to parties and all that but drinking was never really too much my thing. Back then, I really just wanted to work out and do things like that. Drinking wasn't ever really my thing. Partying wasn't ever really my thing neither. I like to read a little bit."

But while Andre was able to resist using drugs or alcohol, the temptation to deal drugs was stronger. Many of his friends had begun dealing crack cocaine, and Andre found it hard not to be impressed by their sudden wealth and a little envious of the things they were able to buy. Not only was there a financial temptation, but his friends were also pressuring him to start dealing too. Today, Andre seems conflicted about which force was stronger—wanting to be part of the popular crowd, or wanting to make money.

Sometimes, Andre says that it was peer pressure that ultimately led to his becoming a small-time crack dealer. While he doesn't want to make excuses for his involvement with crack, he does look back and think that it had a lot to do with his crowd of friends. "I guess I really wanted to be in the in-crowd at the time. . . . So, I guess I was really just trying to hang out with the in-crowd. And I was gone so long, and I came back, and you see people with all this stuff, and it was just enticing . . . peer pressure. That's really the only way I can put it . . . peer pressure."

Other times, Andre thinks that money was the primary factor leading to his years as a crack dealer. Drugs and ostentatious displays of wealth were not as prevalent in Indiana, so when he came back, he was taken with the lifestyle he found many of his old friends caught up in. "That's the only thing that pushed me towards that way, was the money. Some people need to be out there so they need to be accepted, you know? I mean, my mother, she loved me, and my whole family, they loved me. It wasn't to be accepted. It was more to have money and buy things."

Andre began dealing drugs, but always on a small-time basis. He continued to work, and at this point had a job at a furniture store in Queens. In fact, dealing was never Andre's primary source of income. Nevertheless, Andre's involvement in crack, although limited, led to serious, life-altering problems.

Trouble with the Law

Andre was arrested a total of three times over a nine-year period. He insists that each of these arrests were based on false or incorrect charges, but does not blame his convictions or jail time on the police or on unfair racial profiling. He instead places blame squarely on himself for ever having gotten involved with crack in the first place.

Andre's first brush with the law was in 1989 at a community gathering in a local park in Queens, when he was just 17 years old. Although he was involved in dealing, he was not selling drugs at that particular event. "I was doing the wrong thing, but not at this particular time. Another person that was doing the wrong thing had the same exact colors [of clothing] I had. So [the police] came and they picked up all of us with that color on. And they never did find the exact person. But at that particular time they charged me with observation selling, which they charged everybody with."[2]

---

2. An observation sale is when a police officer sees a drug sale take place but does not actually participate in it. See www.nycdefense.com/substances.

The police had seen someone in the park selling crack cocaine. The dealer was described as a young African-American man wearing a red shirt, blue jeans, and red sneakers. There were five men at the party matching this description, and each one of them was arrested for dealing drugs. The police told Andre that he fit the description of the dealer, and he was placed in a van with the four other young men. The police officers didn't find drugs on any of them, but they were all charged with criminal possession. Since Andre was under eighteen at the time, it was considered a "youthful offense," which would disappear from his record as long as he avoided arrest for three years.

As part of his sentencing, the judge encouraged Andre's mother to put him in some kind of program for at-risk youth. She enrolled him in Job Corps,[3] and Andre went upstate to study business operations and pursue his General Equivalency Degree (GED).[4] He was upstate for nearly a year and came back to New York in December 1990.

After completing Job Corps, Andre moved back in with his mother in Queens and started taking classes at Queensborough Community College. Unfortunately, he wasn't committed to school, and found hanging out with his friends much more appealing than going to class. "I mean I got into my friends, and hanging out, and school just wasn't it." Andre was also working at a cement factory in Queens. Despite these responsibilities, he, like many boys his age, spent most of his time with his friends, and

---

3. Job Corps is a free program that helps 16-24 year olds from low-income families gain employment through educational and vocational training.

4. The General Educational Development Test (GED) is a certification test of high-school level academic skill.

often ended up in trouble. "Kept getting myself into trouble. Trouble, trouble, but not nothing like murdering or killing. But I kept getting myself into trouble."

In retrospect, Andre knows that after his first arrest, he should have stopped his involvement with drugs altogether. But he didn't. "It seemed like . . . I don't know, it was like an addiction. Cause the money was so fast . . . it was like an addiction."

Second Arrest

Three years later, Andre was arrested again, seemingly out of the blue. The police picked him up on the day after Christmas, right after his mother had given him some money. "They were saying that they seen me with drugs. But this time once again they never found the drugs. They kept saying that the money in my pocket was marked, but my mother had just gave me money for Christmas. That was my Christmas present.

"When they caught me I was trying to help this lady bring a washing machine in the building. And I was on my way to Jamaica Avenue [a major thoroughfare in Queens], walking up the hill, and they came around the corner . . . they stopped me. Even the lady—the lady came to court and said that 'This young man was helping me.'" Unfortunately, regardless of the fact that that charge was itself baseless, because Andre had a prior drug charge, it was essentially the police's word versus his. "They charged me with criminal possession. And most of my cases, in all of my cases actually, there was never any drugs on my person.

"But from the first incident, it just rolls over, it just rolls over. And my mother came to court and showed the people the pay stub and the receipt and everything, [to prove] that she gave me the money for Christmas. At first I was mad, but, talking to my mother, and she's like, 'This is what happens . . . you did it to yourself, from the first incident, this is what they see you as.' If I get in trouble again, they're not going to be looking at that specific case, they're going to be looking at 'Oh, he did this before.'"

Andre was charged with criminal possession of a controlled substance, a felony offense. He spent eleven months on Riker's Island waiting for the case to go to trial.[4]

It would be understandable if Andre had a certain resentment towards police and the laws that put him behind bars unfairly, but he seems to think that the fact that he was involved with crack dealing at all justifies his imprisonment. In his mind, it doesn't matter that he was innocent in the incidents for which he was actually charged, because he was guilty on a larger level. "I always believe that if you put yourself out for that, that's on you, cause you put yourself out. Like I put myself out the first time, and I continued to do it. I knew what I was doing was wrong, and at any time anything could have happened, but I chose to still do it. I got caught doing it, kept doing it. I mean, I knew the consequences after the first time, so whether it be the law or not, that was my fault, my mistake, I carry that."

Another Alternative

Andre thinks that the judge on the case was sympathetic to his mother, who was a constant presence in the courtroom. "I had

---

4. Riker's Island is the holding jail for those charged with crimes who are awaiting trial or sentencing. It has a particularly notorious reputation in New York City.

a decent judge who kind of fell for my mother more than he fell for me. So, he gave me another alternative." So, as an alternative to more jail time, the judge offered a deal—instead of going to jail Andre could go to a program called Shock in upstate New York for six months. Andre, worried about his mother, decided to accept the alternative. "My mother, she was all stressed out you know, she wasn't eating. She was losing weight, you know, worried about me. So, I just told her, I'm going to take whatever they give me, just to make it go away, man."

Andre went upstate to Shock, a sentencing alternative for non-violent offenders that is frequently compared to military boot camp. He woke up at five in the morning every day, ran several miles, and did tough physical labor for the remainder of the day. While physically demanding, Andre thinks the experience was ultimately positive. "Oh, man. Very, very tough. I got a whole lot out of it. Yeah, I got a whole lot out of it. It was two black DIs [Drill Instructors]. We had two that was from Brooklyn and the rest was like retired Marines, Navy Seals. They were real strict."

Andre remembers one instructor in particular, who made a lasting impression on him. "I had a DI. He was tough on the out-side, but he was real soft on the inside. He took us out to Mt. Platoon and we sit around and talked and everything, and we saw a side of him we hadn't seen before, a caring side. He kind of like loosened up. He was still hard, but I learned a lot from him too. I took a lot from that experience, took a lot. I wish sometimes that I had never come back to New York City. It was my downfall, but things happen, man."

After the six months in the Shock program, Andre came

back to the city determined to end his involvement with drugs. "After that I just said man, I just got to stay away from the streets, I just got to stay away from my friends. Once I came home in 1992, I started boxing in the Golden Gloves, so that kind of kept me healthy. That kept me healthy, away from all the other stuff." In addition to boxing, Andre returned to work at the furniture store.

All in all, things were looking up. After Shock, Andre had stopped dealing altogether and three years later he met Monica, the woman who would be the mother of his children. Monica's father worked in the same neighborhood as Andre's stepfather, and the two met one day while visiting. They became romantically involved, and Monica gave birth to their first child, a daughter, in 1996. She was living in a Queens townhouse with her extended family, and Andre remained with his mother. In 1997, she gave birth to their second daughter.

A Third Arrest

Andre's third and final arrest occurred in 1998, when he was again charged with an observation sale. Ultimately, as in both prior arrests, it came down to Andre's testimony versus the authorities'. And, as Andre knew very well by that point, a kid with a criminal record is unlikely to be more convincing than a police officer. "If it's their word against yours, they're not going to believe you over nothing." This arrest was particularly painful for Andre since he hadn't been involved with drugs since leaving Shock in 1992. "A lot of my friends tease me. They say I must be the unluckiest guy in America.

"That's when I think my past really caught up to me . . . when they arrested me man, I just had a string of bad luck . . . that's what my mother said, you just have a string of bad luck which follows you. They arrested me coming back from the store, man. I had, like a soda and a pack of donuts in the bag . . . and I'm walking from the store, and they just run up on me."

The police officers accused Andre of selling a vial of crack seven blocks from where they arrested him. They canvassed the blocks between where he was arrested and where the deal was alleged to have happened, and in doing so found an empty vial. It was a rough neighborhood, where crack was common, but they nonetheless asserted that the vial had belonged to Andre. Given his prior record, he had little recourse to dispute the charges. "Once again my past caught up to me. I had a string of bad luck, but I mean, kind of like, you got to suck it up man . . . that's what happened, you can't change that."

Andre returned to court and found that the police had brought a crack addict who lived in his neighborhood to the courtroom, saying that she was the woman who had bought the crack from him. "They trying to make this lady say that I was the one that give it to her and all that. They had us in the courtroom. They had me on this side, the lady over there. The lady was like, 'I've never seen this guy. I don't know this guy.' That's what she's telling the judge. . . . 'I don't know this guy.' And I'm telling them, 'I don't know this lady.'"

Despite the fact that both of them denied knowing each other, because of his background Andre had little choice but to take a plea agreement. He also wanted to put the incident behind him as quickly as possible, for his own sake as well as Monica's and his mother's. His lawyer worked out the best deal she thought possible, and Andre spent another ninety days in jail. The period was stressful for everyone, particularly Andre's mother and Monica, who was left alone with the couple's two young daughters. "[Monica] don't show emotion like that, so you have to constantly ask her, what's the matter with her or something like that. I could see it was weighing on her too, though. She lost a lot of weight, and she was coming back and forth to see me. Eventually I told her she didn't have to come that much, so . . . yeah. It was hard."

Andre attributes all of his arrests and imprisonments to his past as a drug dealer and his prior record and expresses concern that he could continue to be accused of breaking the law, even though he hasn't been involved with drugs since 1992. "Once you labeled as something, that's just it, you know. I mean, I'm trying to work to change it now. But I mean, if an incident were to ever happen involving me and the police again, whether it be for anything, it's going to pop up. Some police officers assume you're guilty, just from your past."

A Fresh Start

Following his third arrest, Andre again returned to his mother's apartment in Queens. By now, his two young daughters were growing up and the house where Monica and the girls lived with her family was becoming cramped. It belonged to Monica's grandmother but was also home to many other relatives, who came and went as they needed a place to live. At various points, Monica's aunts, uncles, cousins, brothers, and sisters, many of whom had young children themselves, were living together in the townhouse.

Monica was anxious to get out. Then, adding to the full house, she became pregnant for a third time, and this time gave birth to a son. Monica was collecting public assistance and taking full-time care of the three young children.[5] After his third arrest, Andre was unable to find work, despite his efforts. "Once I got out this time I just kept looking for a job, looking for a job." The furniture store where he had worked previously moved its warehouse to North Carolina, and Andre was unable to find someone willing to hire him. It didn't help that he now had to tell all potential employers about his criminal record. "That, and I didn't know too much about finding a job. I ain't really have the right tools to go about filling out applications and things like that. That was my problem." With three children and no income, the family clearly couldn't afford the upfront costs of renting an apartment. So, on the advice of Monica's friends, the couple went to the Emergency Assistance Unit (EAU).[6]

Entering the Shelter System

Andre didn't think twice about going to the EAU with Monica. "When I thought about it, I told her, 'It's not really up to me. It's your decision.'" Even though they hadn't lived together, Andre felt that it was his responsibility to go through the process with his girlfriend and children. "I didn't feel comfortable letting her go through all that with three kids by herself, that's how I came

5. Public assistance and welfare are used interchangeably; both refer to the federal entitlement program Temporary Assistance for Needy Families (TANF).
6. The Emergency Assistance Unit is the gateway to the City shelter system.

into the situation. I went through everything with her, even though I didn't have to."

He didn't, however, realize just what he was getting into. "I'm pretty sure she knew what was coming—I didn't know what was coming. I mean, I was there for [the kids] so, I mean . . . I wasn't going to leave at any time. I stuck it out. I just kept telling myself every day I'm doing it for my kids. It's nothing, I mean, if you got that kind of focus, it's nothing. Take the good with the bad, that's what I'm saying."

The family was at the EAU for three days, at which point Andre grew frustrated and concerned about his daughter. "My oldest daughter, she has asthma real bad, and she can't be confined in them kind of places like that. So, I went down there and I explained to them, and I had to take her to the doctor and the doctor gave us a note."

The family went to a welfare motel in Brooklyn while they were being assessed.[7] "It was real bad. It was just real bad . . . a bad place." Like too many other families, their ten-day assessment period stretched to three months. Monica collected welfare, and Andre, still unable to secure a job, got help from his family. "I had family, man. They helped me out a lot. And then my situation, they understood it."

After three months, Andre, Monica, and the children were

7. Welfare hotels are a form of temporary housing for homeless families. The City leases blocks of rooms in hotels at a greater cost than Tier II shelters, but the hotels do not offer supportive services and they are notorious for drug use, substandard cleanliness, and criminal activity. The application for shelter involves a 10-day assessment period during which families stay in a conditional placement. While applying for shelter at the Emergency Assistance Unit (EAU) or the Prevention Assistance and Temporary Housing (PATH) office families are required to provide the names and addresses of all residences from the two years preceding homelessness. Caseworkers then call or visit these residences to determine whether or not families may return there. Despite 10-day limits, assessment periods can, and often do, last for weeks.

sent to a larger and more comprehensive transitional shelter in Queens. "It was better in a lot of ways for us. I mean, we both from Queens, so our families is just down the block. A bus ride is right down the block, so it's not far. So that was a lot of good. I probably say I benefited more than anybody."

Shelter

The shelter proved pivotal for the family—and eventually Andre started working in the very same recreation department his children played in while they were living there. "I had people out there that helped me out a whole lot. We had, like a case manager, she was great. I benefited a lot. And then, actually it was her that spoke to my supervisor about me getting the position that I got now. I'll be honest with you, I don't know where I'd be if somebody like her . . . you know . . . I can't speak for all of the case managers, but you know, she cared, she cared a whole lot. That's what happens when people care."

Meanwhile, Monica began taking business classes at a trade school, which was also helping her get her GED. Unfortunately, she had a difficult time handling the pressures of a family and school. "She couldn't do everything and go to school." Monica had also found complications with her financial aid package. "They saying that she had to take out student loans. She wasn't willing to do that, not for the money they were saying she had to take out for. So she stopped doing that."

Still, the children were doing well and attended the shelter's daycare center. The staff of the shelter's recreation center got to know Andre as well. He often visited the recreation space, and volunteered to help out. His extensive athletic experience was a great asset, and soon Andre was offered a part-time job. It was June of 2001. By the fall, the family had been approved for a Section 8 housing subsidy and Monica found them an apartment on Bushwick Avenue, in Brooklyn.[8] Three months after moving out, Andre was offered a full-time position at the recreation center.

A New Home

Andre and his family lived in the Bushwick apartment for two years. Monica worked here and there when she could, and gave birth to another daughter. In 2002, Andre and Monica were officially married. "Things was going good. I had kids, and I just thought it was right."

In late 2003, Andre and Monica started having trouble in their marriage. They have since split up, and each is back living doubled up with their families. Andre doesn't talk very much about their separation, and it's apparent that it's a difficult subject for him. "We kind of like, goin' on different paths, so you know, that's part of life. Things happen. I just say that sometimes people just grow apart. What seems right ten years earlier, ten years later people are on different pages. One person wants to go this way, one person wants to go that way. It's not going to work like that."

Neither Monica nor Andre has made any move towards getting a divorce, however. "I don't think we both want that. I mean, we not talking about that." Instead the two remain separated, and are hoping to work things out. Meanwhile, Andre is living

---

8. Section 8 is a federal housing subsidy for low-income renters that pays the difference between 30 percent of the renters' incomes and the fair market rent.

with his mother and trying to save money for another apartment.

Today

Andre continues to work for the recreation program at the shelter. "I love my job, love my job. The kids, man . . . I could be, like, down, coming to work. But when I see that one kid. I play with these kids, I run around with them, we do a lot of things. So, they make it worthwhile for me to come to work. Just one kid, just one kid. That's all it takes. Cause I can usually walk into the building and that one kid sees me and we start talking, and I know that I work there . . . it's a great thing."

Andre says that his job at the recreation program is the most rewarding one he's ever had. "I never knew how much work it took, and I never knew the rewards you get out of it. It's not monetary gain, it's not anything, it's just . . . I mean, I coach the football team right now and we like . . . we 4 and 0, and we like, basically, we blow everybody out. And I get a reward from seeing these kids, because we practice a lot, they work hard, and that's my reward."

He also sees it as a way of giving back and making up for some of the damage he might have done during his days as a crack dealer. "I mean, doing what I did, I knew I contributed to help ruin a couple of lives. That's not a good thing. That's not good for people's mother, people's father. For a while, I was contributing to that. And this is kind of like my reward. I'm giving something back. That's how I look at it. I'm giving it back, I'm giving it back."

Looking Forward

In 2005, Andre started taking college level classes in human services at a local community college. He's planning to major in Human Services Administration, but his ultimate goal is simply to have a positive impact in his community. "I just want to be one of the decision-makers in what happens. Because a lot of things that's going on, say with the kids, for instance, decisions could be a whole lot different. They could make the situation better for them, but [they're] not. I think there's not enough outlets for young kids nowadays, that's why they turn to the gangs and the drugs. Especially like in the areas [where] I grew up, it's not enough. I hope I could try to change something."

In the spring of 2005, Andre was taking four classes and working full-time. He admits that he's tired most of the time, but thinks it's worth it to get his degree completed as quickly as he can. Unfortunately, his busy schedule leaves him little time with his children.

Andre will likely never escape the stigma and obstacles of having had a felony conviction. He is not allowed to live in public housing, and every time he applies for a job he has to tell his potential employer about his conviction. Some opportunities are simply not open to him because of his past. "It affects a lot. To be honest with you, I check into what I'm going to do before I do it. I look at common stipulations. If they state that you can't have a criminal record, I leave it alone. I don't dwell on that. There's nothing I can do, I can't change that."

Although Andre is no longer homeless, he continues to work in the shelter's recreation program. Attending cultural events, playing games, and having the chance to just enjoy being a kid is of critical importance when a child is homeless. After seeing the way the recreation program helped his own children, Andre has become a committed, enthusiastic, and beloved staff member at the shelter's program.

CHAPTER FIVE

Theresa

Overcoming Addiction

I'm not blaming the projects, but I mean, it was all over. It was everywhere I turned. Crack to the right of me! Crack to the left of me! You know, it was everywhere.

To say that Theresa is big-hearted does not do her justice. She wraps her arms, metaphorically and literally, around everyone. As we sit talking in the break room of the family shelter where she works as a security guard, Theresa beams, enthusiastically welcoming the young mothers and children who trickle in through the door. She is the shelter's self-appointed cheerleader, and has a smile, a hug, and an encouraging word for everyone she sees. Theresa tells her story carefully and chronologically, describing the periods when she struggled with addiction with uncanny self-awareness, not once losing her trademark warmth, openness, and strength.

Childhood in Mouse Corner

Little about Theresa's childhood foreshadows her later years as a crack addict living in some of New York's most notorious housing projects. Her mother was eighteen years old and unmarried when she gave birth to Theresa. They lived with Theresa's grandmother and three cousins in a small town in South Carolina, worlds away from urban inner-city life. "It was a little town called Mouse Corner. You could run right through it. Before you know it, you're out of it."

When Theresa was three years old, her mother, frustrated by the lack of job opportunities in Mouse Corner, decided to move to Boston. "She wasn't making [enough] money to take care of me. She was too young. My father was still down there, but I didn't see him much. That's another reason why my mother left. She said he wasn't really helping out and she wasn't going to sit around and wait for him to throw money at her whenever he felt like it." Theresa was left behind with her grandmother and for the next nine years she rarely saw her mother. Still, she remembers those years fondly. "I wasn't really mad at her or anything like that. To be honest with you, it was always Grandma. I don't really remember my mother being there when I was little, but she said she was there."

Moving North

When Theresa was twelve, her world turned upside down. In Boston, her mother had met and married a man, and together they decided to move to New York. Once they were settled in Brooklyn, they sent for Theresa. Reluctantly, she went. "At first I didn't really want to leave my grandmother, you know. I got really attached to her, but my mother was like, 'Your place is with me.' So I came up here."

76

Initially, Theresa had trouble adjusting to her new environment. The city was unfamiliar and intimidating for a girl from rural South Carolina. "I didn't really care for New York. . . . People are mean up here! Thank God for the summer—I used to go down and stay with my grandmother. So thank God for that." Spending summers with her grandmother in South Carolina was the one constant in Theresa's life as she slowly acclimated to the new city, her new stepfather, and living with her mother. Her grandmother's death, however, changed everything.

"As I got older, the apartment that we had was too small. My grandmother passed away. So all my other cousins had to come up and stay with us too, until their mothers decided to take them [back]." Theresa's three cousins moved up to New York, two younger boys and Jennifer, who is just a year older than Theresa. "When my mother took her [in], it was really like she was my sister. We were raised that way."

Theresa and her new extended family moved to a larger apartment in Far Rockaway, Queens, halfway through her freshman year of high school. It was a particularly difficult transition for the fifteen-year-old. "That was really rough for me. The way they run things, everything's different. The school was so big. And nobody's showing you, nobody's taking time out." She didn't know the school's layout, frequently got lost, and was consequently often late for class. "By the time I got to class, everybody's sitting down, and I'm looking in there, and I'm like, I'm not walking in there!" Theresa would never fully recover academically from the stress of changing schools midway through the year.

Job Corps

In the meantime, Theresa's cousin Jennifer had decided that she didn't want to go to a traditional high school but instead enroll in Job Corps, a residential job-training program in upstate New York. Theresa, on the other hand, was hoping to finish high school. But one afternoon, Theresa's mother came home early and found the girls with boys in the house. This was against the family rules, and as punishment, Theresa's mother sent her upstate to Job Corps with Jennifer.

In Job Corps, Theresa studied nursing in preparation to become a home health aide. While she and Jennifer remained close upstate, Theresa kept her distance as Jennifer ran with a rough crowd. Soon enough, Jennifer had started experimenting with drugs; before long, she developed a problem with speed and amphetamines.

After six months in Job Corps, the girls came home for Christmas, and Jennifer had a breakdown. "She bugged out. Crying, laughing. She was wacko; she couldn't go back up there."

Now, Theresa thinks that Jennifer's breakdown was probably caused by latent mental illness. "What my mother came to realize is that, in a way, [Jennifer] was already a little off. And the speed just helped it along." Jennifer was the youngest of seven children, and her mother, although undiagnosed, was probably mentally ill herself. "I mean, that's our cousin, but [Jennifer's mother] was off. And she just kept having babies. And after a while they just started treating the babies like puppies. She couldn't keep track of who her kids were." Eventually, Jennifer ended up in a mental hospital, and has been in and out of institutions and on various medications to this day.

At the end of the Christmas holiday, Theresa returned to Job Corps alone. It was a bittersweet trip; Theresa was upset about Jennifer's condition, but also a little relieved to be out of her older cousin's shadow. "I was sad at the time because I didn't want nothing like that to happen to her. But I was happy that I was going back to Job Corps by myself. I'm an only child but I never felt like an only child because I always had my cousins and them there. So going up to Job Corps for me was a big thing."

Despite her initial reservations about going to Job Corps, once Theresa was back upstate on her own, she found that she enjoyed it. She was comfortable in rural New York, felt fulfilled by what she was learning, and was proud of her accomplishments. "I liked it! I accomplished a lot from Job Corps. They really do pay you for learning. I got my GED.[1] I graduated, and my mother came up for the ceremony."

Back in New York City

After graduation, Theresa returned to her family's home in New York City. She had found work as a home health aide, but the position involved a nearly two-hour commute from Far Rockaway to her clients in the Bronx and Harlem. "They didn't have many clients for me, and I didn't mind. I'm still young, I'm hanging out, I'm done with Job Corps now, I need this break."

Theresa also resumed friendships with some of the people she knew before she went upstate, and started to experiment with

---

1. The General Educational Development Test (GED) is a certification test of high-school level academic skill.

drugs. "It's just me at home, trying to do the adult thing. I'm nineteen. I go to work. [Then] I was introduced to marijuana. So I'm smoking weed now, hanging out."

Things at work changed once she started getting paid. "This is how I found out that my mother is very greedy. My first check was sixty-six dollars. And you know how much my mother wanted? Fifty dollars. So I was like, you know? This is not working out. So I quit the job. Because I wasn't going to give my mother all that money. I mean, c'mon. I'm working hard!"

After she quit working as a home health aide, Theresa's stepfather helped her get a job wrapping Christmas presents at a department store in Manhattan. This time, she had learned a lesson. She worked seven days a week, but kept her earnings a secret from her mother. "It was good because I was getting the money and then I was telling her I was getting less. Because I knew how my mother was now, so I knew I had to be way ahead of her. What do they say? Never let the right hand know what the left hand is doing. It was like that with my mom."

Terrence

The following year, Theresa's life took another unexpected turn. At twenty, she accidentally became pregnant by her first boyfriend, a young man named Terrence whom she met through a neighbor. Her mother encouraged her to have an abortion, but she was adamant in her decision not to terminate the pregnancy, partly because of a previous abortion she had kept secret. "She wasn't ready for me to get pregnant, but it happened, and I wasn't going to get an abortion. I never told her, but I had got pregnant in Job

Corps. That was my first abortion in life. I never told her. I kept it to myself. So this time I was like, I'm not doing that; I'm not getting no abortion. If it happens, it happens."

Now pregnant, and her seasonal job at the department store over, Theresa's aunt helped her get a position as a security guard at a shelter for homeless families. It was similar to the position she holds today, albeit in an entirely different kind of facility. "It was not a shelter where you had your own rooms—it was bed, bed, bed. That's how the shelters used to be, you see. There was no room, no privacy."

Theresa gave birth to a son and named him Laurence. For a while they lived with her mother, but soon the stress of so many people and an infant under one roof grew to be too much, and Theresa decided it was time to leave.

Her relationship with Terrence had been rocky, and during her pregnancy the two broke up. "He told me he needed 'time,'" she says, rolling her eyes. In response to their breakup, and in an effort to gain independence, Theresa applied for public housing.[2] "I'm going to do what I have to do. So I went to Housing, and they called me for Queensbridge Houses in Long Island City." This assignment proved unfortunate: that particular housing project was so infested with crack cocaine that it was notorious throughout the city. "I didn't know it was the 'crack capital.' But I'm not going to blame Queensbridge [Houses]."

---

2. Public housing is administered by the New York City Housing Authority (NYCHA), an agency that provides affordable housing throughout the five boroughs of New York City. NYCHA administers the majority of the City's affordable housing stock, including the "housing projects."

The Crack Capital

Shortly after Theresa moved into the housing project, she befriended another young mother with a similar background and situation. "We had our sons around the same time so you could say they grew up together. And I thought she was really cool. She introduced me to this crack cocaine. She said 'You put it in weed, you do it like that.' But she went to higher levels. She started doing the pipe. I knew she started changing and going for the worse because my son's bracelet was missing, and she was the last one with him. She denied it, and I knew that I'd waste time if I beat her up. Fight her, still ain't got the bracelet. My point was to leave her alone. She was gone. I was looking for her one day cause she owed me some money, and she was under the stairs with a pipe in her hand."

Despite witnessing her friend's spiraling addiction to crack, Theresa continued to experiment with drugs, but at this point, she claims she was still under control. In the meantime, she and Terrence reconciled and he moved into the apartment with her and their son.

For a while, things were starting to look up. Terrence was working steadily, and the three were living together as a family in their own home. Still, Theresa continued to occasionally use drugs. And although Terrence stayed away from crack, he dabbled in cocaine and drank frequently on the weekends.

After Laurence's birth, Theresa took a maternity leave, but once she moved into the projects, she decided not to return to work at all. Instead, she stayed home with her infant son and collected public assistance.[3] "Got on welfare, it helped me pay my rent. So, I got lazy and dependent strictly on public assistance. Waiting patiently for them two weeks for the check to come. That was my job. That's how welfare recipients get, I'm telling you."

Theresa struggled with a growing addiction, a lack of work, and a faltering relationship. "I guess living with him, I got to really see who he was . . . sometimes a little nasty, a little cold. And I guess he didn't know who I really was either. At first it started out good, and then, I don't know, I started getting real depressed, just dealing with him. I mean, he was there, but he wasn't there. [I was] just lonely. So I started smoking even more. Never with the pipe, always with the weed. But it don't matter how you rationalize it—crack is crack no matter how you smoke it. It was getting worse every day, but I didn't realize it."

Depressed, dependent on public assistance, and plagued by an escalating crack habit, things were getting progressively worse. "Eventually, I started letting myself go, like cleaning the house, having food on the table. . . . Eventually [Terrence] started to complain, you know 'When I come home, the dishes aren't clean, the food ain't on the table. I'm leaving.' But when he left, I even smoked more."

After Terrence

Once Terrence moved out, Theresa was a single parent again, only now she had a serious crack habit and a growing young son, Laurence. Before long, she started sending Laurence to her mother's house so that she could stay home and smoke crack-laced

---

3. Public assistance and welfare are used interchangeably; both refer to the federal entitlement program Temporary Assistance for Needy Families (TANF).

marijuana. Her rent was being paid directly by welfare, and her life was spiraling out of control. Soon another unexpected life turn would add to her precarious situation.

While she was living at Queensbridge Houses, Theresa would periodically pass a construction site. There, she met a man named Dean. Theresa's struggles left her barely able to form a romantic or emotional connection, but nevertheless, she and Dean became sexually involved, partly because of her growing addiction.

"I didn't really love this man. But at the time I was getting high, so I saw his wallet. You know, big wallet, more drugs! That's what I thought. But we got together, and I ended up pregnant." Still actively using crack cocaine, Theresa denied her pregnancy for months because she did not want anyone to say anything about her drug use and the possibility that she was harming the fetus. Eventually, it was too late to seek an abortion.

At the same time that she was pregnant with her second child, her cousin Jennifer, still in and out of mental institutions, became pregnant as well. Theresa's instinct was to offer to raise Jennifer's child herself, since no one in the family thought that Jennifer was competent enough to be a parent. "We've got to think about what's best for the child. But I'm pregnant, denying I'm pregnant, and high on drugs. What the hell am I going to do with a child? But, we were trying to do that so the child wouldn't get in the [child welfare] system."

Despite their concerns, Theresa's family ultimately put Jennifer's child in foster care; in the end, against all odds, it was a good decision. "God watches over us, I'm telling you. Cause she just happened to have the most wonderful, most beautiful foster mother there is."

The experience helped Theresa come to terms with her own pregnancy and begin to gain perspective on her addiction. Although she had anticipated losing her baby if the doctors found drugs in his system, miraculously, he was clean, and she was able to bring her newborn son, Thomas, home with her. "So I got my baby, and it's time for me to get my shit together. I had Laurence, you know, so, you think that stopped me? No. My mom would take him on the weekend, and I'd do my thing. And then after a while I started leaving the baby with Laurence in the house and going out." At the time, Laurence was six years old.

Hitting Bottom

Although the uncertainty surrounding Thomas's birth helped her realize that she had a problem, Theresa was still powerless to her addiction and not yet ready to overcome it on her own. It would take outside threats and clear danger to her children to convince her to seek help.

Theresa's neighbor and drug dealer was abusive toward his wife, who happened to be a close friend of hers. "When a woman's being beat by a man, and you get involved, do you know that both of them will turn on you? So sometimes it's good to not say anything, just mind your business." Angry about Theresa's meddling, her dealer contacted her mother and told her about Theresa's escalating drug use and the fact that she sometimes left her infant son in the care of his brother. Alarmed, her mother threatened to call the Administration for Children's Services [ACS] if Theresa didn't check herself into a rehabilitation program.

But ultimately, it was concern for her children's future well-being that convinced her to seek treatment. Crack was rampant at the Queensbridge Houses, and drug dealers had begun enlisting children as low-level drug runners. "Thank God my kids were still young. Cause these guys wanted to recruit children now." Theresa knew it was no place to raise her sons; the time had come for her to leave Queensbridge and seek treatment. "Let me go into a program. I didn't want to go into an outreach. Outreach is where you go there and then you come home. Okay, so after I come home, I out-reach for more drugs. I knew that couldn't work." She decided to give up her apartment and enter a residential drug treatment program.

Available apartments in city housing projects are few and far between, and families often end up waiting years to be placed there. Theresa's decision to leave her New York City Housing Authority (NYCHA) apartment was rare, but she felt like it was the right thing to do. "I went to Housing, and I told them my situation. I told them I was going to give up my apartment. The man looked at me and said, 'Wow, you don't hear that very often.' People are always trying to make a deal or something or sublet the apartment to a friend. A few people asked me, a few people I used to get high with asked me. But I knew the route I was going, so I knew where they were going right behind me! I was like, 'You're not going to mess up my name.'"

Theresa left her children with her mother and entered a drug treatment program in upstate New York. "I said, 'Yeah, Ma, I can do this.' I cried and everything. I kissed my babies. I said, 'Ma, take care of my babies.' And then I walked down there with my bags and stuff and signed up." Six years had passed since she first entered the "crack capital" of New York.

Seeking Treatment

Theresa entered treatment in Dutchess County, where she stayed for a year and seven months. "At first I didn't really feel it, I was just going through the motions. 'Yeah, yeah, yeah, the philosophy, blah, blah, blah.' But the counselors know that, because that's what they're trained to do. So they see that, and that's why they kept me up there as long as they did. And when they let me go, you better believe I was ready. And I can say, to this day, I haven't touched any drugs."

Theresa was finally on the path toward recovery, when the custody of her children was threatened. While Theresa was upstate, her stepfather passed away, and her mother was forced to move out of their home into a smaller apartment. Her mother also started drinking heavily. "My mother was calling up [the drug treatment program] talking to the counselors drunk." Concerned for the welfare of Theresa's children, her counselors called ACS and reported her mother's behavior. "It just so happens that when ACS does come, my mother's drunk. So they took the kids. I'm in treatment and I'm bugging out. I can't touch them, I can't hold them."

ACS staff allowed Theresa to meet with them before her children were officially entered in the system. She traveled downstate and asked the boys' fathers to watch them for the remainder of the time she was in treatment; both agreed. "Okay, my problem now is I've got to get out of [the drug treatment program]. I've got to get off my ass and get my kids. That's what motivated me."

Theresa was particularly concerned about her younger son. Thomas's father was living with a woman who disliked Theresa. "She hates me so she's taking it out on my son. Putting cigarettes out on my baby and stuff like that."

A Fresh Start

A year and a half after entering rehab, Theresa completed the program, returned to New York City, and moved back in with her mother and two young sons. She again applied for public housing, but she knew that it could take time, if it came through at all. Meanwhile, her mother continued to abuse alcohol and refused to seek treatment, despite Theresa's persistent requests. Not wanting to subject her children to more substance abuse with a longer stay in their alcoholic grandmother's home, she was anxious to leave the apartment.

Unfamiliar with the City shelter system, she packed her bags and took her children to her local welfare office. "I went to welfare, and I told them that I was homeless and everything and I just planted myself right there. That's when they saw that I was serious." The public assistance office put Theresa and her children in a taxi headed to the Emergency Assistance Unit (EAU) in the Bronx.[4]

Entering the System

At the EAU, Theresa was denied emergency shelter ten times. "That's what they do to try to get you to give up and go someplace else. Just to see if you're serious. Well, damn. After ten

---

4. The Emergency Assistance Unit is the gateway to the City shelter system.

times y'all [still] don't believe me?"

Theresa soon found help—she was introduced to a lawyer willing to take on homeless clients pro bono, and she was ultimately given a "fair hearing," a court proceeding in which an individual can challenge a decision made by a city agency. "My excuses [for being homeless] were valid . . . but they wanted me to give up. And I didn't, and I called [the lawyer] and I gave her all the information, everything I went through, all the documents. I showed them how they turned me down. And she said, 'You're going to come here, you're going to do what you've got to do for yourself, and then you're going to move out.'"

After being placed in a ten-day conditional placement,[5] Theresa was told that she and her children would be moved to a Tier II transitional housing family shelter; she was ecstatic.[6] "All we wanted to hear was Tier II. Tier II means stay put, no more moving. I didn't care where it was. It could be Timbuktu. I don't care. Me and my kids was going; we didn't have to be bothered with EAU again."

Support System

Fortunately, Theresa and her sons were taken to a Tier II shelter that offered extensive supportive services—job training programs, GED classes, parenting workshops, day care, and

---

5. The application for shelter involves a 10-day assessment period during which families stay in a conditional placement. While applying for shelter at the Emergency Assistance Unit (EAU) or the Prevention Assistance and Temporary Housing (PATH) intake center families are required to provide the names and addresses of all residences from the two years preceding homelessness. Caseworkers then call or visit these residences to determine whether or not families may return there. Despite 10-day limits, assessment periods can, and often do, last for weeks.

6. Tier II Shelters are nonprofit operated facilities for homeless families with children 18 or younger.

women's groups, among others. "They explained to me so many things. 'Oh, we got parenting skills, women's groups . . . then I started seeing there were interns. I saw women in security suits and ladies as porters. Then I'd see them go in their rooms and change, so I was checking all that out and I said, 'Security? That's my field!'" Theresa approached her caseworker and was quickly hired for an internship as a security guard.

From her first trip to the EAU, through her fight to gain acceptance into the New York City shelter system, and throughout her stay at the Tier II family shelter in Queens, Theresa attended substance abuse support group meetings every Wednesday. After school, Laurence and Thomas would go to her mother's house so that she could do her internship at the shelter and take care of housing applications. Theresa also went to daily women's groups, signed up for a job skills program, and brought her children to school in Far Rockaway every morning. "I didn't want them to stop going to school. No way. I was getting up at 4:30, 5:00, but I didn't have to sit there and look miserable. I had stuff to do. I kept them motivated. They didn't have time to think of being sad and 'Oh, Mom. We're homeless.' We was moving all the time."

Within a few months, Theresa had become the shelter's de facto cheerleader. "I did all the little groups. Finished it. Got other people to sign up for them. 'Yeah, we got women's group—we have so much fun! We watch movies . . . parenting is good, it lets you know . . . how to talk to your kids.' Yeah so I was bringing in other people. So the groups were getting kind of full. They was looking nice and healthy. We loved it.

"There were some good people here, put it that way. A lot

of them are doing good now. Some work for the City, some for the state, Jamaica Hospital. I seen them doing real good. So if [someone] were to ask me if I knew someone who got something good from [the shelter], I'd say 'Hell, yeah! Hell, yeah.'"

Theresa's security internship required 240 hours of work, which she completed after nine months. Instead of stopping when she fulfilled her hours, Theresa continued to work as a security guard for no compensation. "Nine months [I] gave them free of my time. Cause after that, [my caseworker] came to me, said, 'You went over your 240 hours, and you still gave time. They're going to hire you. You're going to be full-time.' I'll never forget it."

A New Home

At around the same time that she found employment, Theresa's application for public housing was approved. "They didn't let me go to Queens. They picked Brooklyn. They said, 'Let's try a new borough for her, the girl done went through treatment.'" First, Theresa was shown an apartment in a Brooklyn project. "The apartment was nice. I liked the way it was made and everything. It was only on the second floor. But I didn't like the little drug-heads hanging under my window. I could see me now arguing with them, 'Please get away from my window.'"

Theresa felt nervous about rejecting the apartment, mostly because she feared that the Housing Authority might not be willing to give her another choice. "Like I said, it's how you talk to people. Sometimes they can send you right back to the same place and if you turn it down, that's it. I told [the woman at the Housing Authority], I said, 'I lived in Queensbridge, and I gave it up.' I said, 'Too drug infested. I got my kids; I want them to go to church. I'm a good person, I believe in God, I enforce it in my children, and this is not a good area for me and my children, honestly.' And she saw my disposition and she said to me, 'I don't think so either, sweetheart. I think you can get something better.' So she took my hand, we shook and everything, next thing I know, a week later, they called me for Canarsie.[7] Thank God, Canarsie was the place. And I took my kids and said, 'Let's go check it out,' and they loved it."

Life Today

Theresa has been working full-time at the shelter and living with her two sons in Canarsie for eight years. She loves her new neighborhood in East Brooklyn and feels much safer there than she did in the Queensbridge projects. "I see the cops up and down Flatlands [Avenue]. I'm glad to see them, up and down, that's right! Keep my block nice and tight!"

Three years ago, Theresa met a man named Robert and cautiously started dating him. They'd been seeing each other for a year and a half when she became pregnant for a third time, this time with a daughter the couple named Terri Lynn. Shortly after her birth, they were married.

Just as Theresa seemed to have hit a lucky streak, she and her husband hit a rough patch. "We got married. As soon as we got married, bam! The job let him go." For the first year of her daughter's life, she worked at the shelter while Robert stayed home with the baby. "After a while it got kind of hard because it was all on

7. Canarsie is a neighborhood in Brooklyn.

me. To come home from work, and then to cook, it takes a lot from you. And since he's in the house now, there's no leftovers! No. . . . I've got to cook every day now. And then take care of the baby. "He's a good provider. I have faith in him. You know? So I held on and I waited. I said, we're going to find something. We're not going to give up." Fortunately, after a year of unemployment, Theresa helped Robert find a job with a construction company through friends of hers from work.

Now, Theresa, Robert, her two sons, and their daughter live together in Canarsie. She is anxious not to make the same mistakes with her new daughter that she regrets making with her sons. "Both of my kids are in Special Ed. When I was on drugs, I didn't take up time enough to sit down with my kids and read more. That's why you learn from your mistakes. Cause I'm totally the opposite now. 'C'mon, let's read a book! C'mon, c'mon. We're reading a book!' Yeah, I didn't do that then, but I'm damn sure making sure I do it now. More so than ever. Cause I didn't take the time out and I should have.

"One thing that I promised myself is that I would make sure they get their education. Because when I was on drugs, it was like I didn't care. I was busy trying to get high. I was invested more in that. They're in Special Ed now, and I can blame myself." But while Theresa feels responsible for her sons' academic difficulties, she also resents that the blame is placed entirely on her. "It was like everything was on the woman to do. It's like to this day with Laurence's father, we'll get into it and he'll say certain things, 'Well, you know whose fault that is.' Yeah, yeah, yeah. 'You saying it's me, but what did you do to help? What did you do when you had

Laurence? Did you teach him how to read? Because you can't tell me nothing because you didn't help.' So neither one of us did anything. We both at fault. Okay, you want to put it more on me to make you feel good, fine. I don't care. I already carry that baggage; I already know what I did. And I'm rectifying it. I'm trying anyway."

Laurence and Thomas both speak to their fathers, but neither of the boys is particularly close to his dad. "Laurence, I told his father to spend more time with him. Yeah, you talk on the phone, you throw a little money his way, but a child needs that attention. A child needs that time. A child needs that man-to-man talk. He didn't give him that. Now he's calling constantly." Although Laurence's father now makes a much greater effort to see him and be in contact with him, Laurence is eighteen years old and busy with sports, friends, and school, and shows little interest in trying to develop a relationship with his father. He does have a very specific goal in mind—when he and his family were homeless, he attended a summer camp run by the shelter, and this summer he's hoping to return to the camp to work as a counselor.

Today, in talking about her position at the shelter, Theresa recalls her own time as a resident, and tries to emulate the example set for her. "I do what they did for me, cause I know how it made me feel comfortable. Okay, make the child feel comfortable, that puts the mother at ease. They explained to me so many things. Now they say 'If it wasn't for you, I'd be scared. But you made me feel comfortable. With your smile and your friendliness.'" Recognizing the strength of her story, Theresa's bosses routinely ask her to sit at the shelter's front desk, so that hers is the first face people see when they walk through the door.

Looking Forward

Theresa's great-grandmother was a midwife in South Carolina, and in lieu of cash, many of her clients paid her in land. Some of this land was passed on to Theresa. "My plan is to some-day get me a house. I have land down South. Just to save money to get a house on it. That's what I'm working on now.

"I want that picket fence. I want that big yard. My eight-een-year-old is a little too big now to run in the yard. But he can play with his little brother and his little sister out there on the lawn. That's my dream."

Theresa's dream of a yard and a white picket fence in South Carolina is a long way from the reality of her years as a drug addict in the Queensbridge projects. But seeing how far she's come, it certainly seems within reach. Theresa has not smoked crack cocaine since she went to treatment, and to this day she remains clean. Often, events like a spouse's loss of employment or an unplanned pregnancy are enough to plunge a struggling family back into homelessness—especially when those events coincide. But Theresa persevered through that difficult period and kept her family intact, all the while staying sober and positive.

In the meantime, Theresa continues to do her best to motivate the women she sees every day who are facing the same challenges she faced so many years ago. "I hope the little informa-tion I've given you will help to motivate a lot of other people. Believe me, I'm not just doing it here. I talk to them personally. So, I'm motivating a few. I'm doing a little bit. It's hard to push, but

I'm doing it."

She continues to greet each incoming family at the shelter with warmth and compassion, and despite her struggles, she is positive and hopeful for her and own family's future. "I have a lot of obstacles, but let me tell you something, I will not let nothing get me down, cause it could be worse."

———————————————————

The job readiness training and internship programs at the shelter where Theresa was assigned gave her the necessary skills to find gainful employment that would allow her to reach her goals for her family and herself. In addition, Theresa's internship at the shelter provided her with valuable on-the-job training that proved indispensable when it came time to look for future positions.

CHAPTER SIX
Monique

Homeless Once, Homeless Again

I always said that I'm going to make my mother a liar— that I am going to be somebody. I am going to do something with my life, and I'm going to be a better mother than she ever was.

Sitting with Monique in the shelter where she works, there's hardly a moment of silence or privacy. The shelter is bustling with young women, and most of them stop as soon as they see Monique, eager to ask for advice about their children or boyfriends. When one after another comes through the room, Monique rolls her eyes. "I just have one of those faces that people just stop and want to talk to. And half of them I don't know." Heavy-set and quick to laugh, Monique has an easy and amiable warmth. Most remarkably, she retains her sunny disposition throughout our interviews, focusing on the positive even when describing the horrific abuse that marked her youth in Brooklyn, and the gunshot wound that could have taken her life.

PART I

Daddy's Girl

Monique's parents met when her father was in his forties and her mother was just eighteen. A young model from an abusive household, Monique's mother quickly fell in love with the older World War II veteran and soon moved out of her parents' house and in with him. Despite the twenty-seven-year age difference, the relationship would produce five children and last twenty-seven years, until Monique's father's death in 1989.

She recalls her earliest childhood years fondly, remembering a close relationship with her father and siblings. Of five children, Monique was the second; she has one older sister, two younger sisters, and a younger brother. Her two older half-brothers from her father's previous relationship lived with their mother in another neighborhood in Brooklyn. Monique's mother was a full-time homemaker; her father collected a pension from his time in the service and was the superintendent of the building in which they lived. He would also fix broken things he found and either sell them to people in the neighborhood or keep them for his own family. "He would just bring junk in and fix it! We had so much junk in the house. Once, we had two TV's that were exactly the same; one had the sound, one had the picture."

Monique describes herself as a "daddy's girl" and she inherited her father's knack for tinkering and fixing things. But while she admired him a great deal, she also describes him as a "functional alcoholic," whose drinking frequently prompted arguments between him and her mother. "He always paid the bills first and whatever chump change he had left, that's when he would drink.

[Then] he'd come home and want to argue and stuff, and she didn't like it."

Despite the drinking and arguments, Monique thinks he was basically a great father. "He was always a good father, a good provider. I hated when they argued, or if he didn't come home, but most of the time he was always there. He always helped me with my homework; he always tried to guide us in the right direction. And he was just fun to be around. It wasn't like he'd drink every single day. He was like the coolest. Wherever he went, I wanted to go. We had so much fun together."

Monique and her father's close relationship may have been in part because of her mother's clear preference for Monique's siblings. "Growing up, most people always saw how she always treated me differently. Like she wouldn't buy me clothes or she wouldn't, you know, do certain things with me. And I never knew why. And I used to always ask like, 'What did I do so wrong that makes you treat me so bad?' And she would never answer that question. Never."

Years later, Monique would find out that she and her next younger sister resembled their maternal grandmother, who had been abusive to their mother, and it was unresolved feelings over this abuse that accounted for her mother's unfair treatment. At this point, however, Monique only knew that her mother had "picks," and that she wasn't one of them.

As a young child, Monique wasn't terribly concerned with her mother's favoritism, since she felt closer to her father anyway. "She had 'picks,' but I didn't care because I was a daddy's girl." But then her father became ill with cancer. Recognizing her compe-

99

tence and sense of responsibility, Monique's father began teaching her how to take care of things around the house. "When he got really sick he sent me to start doing food shopping, he taught me how to cook. My mother didn't know how to do hair and there were all these girls in the house. So I learned how to do hair, learned how to do laundry. He taught me so much, because these were the things that my mother didn't know how to do, because my grandmother never taught her. So, he knew that he was dying, and he taught me so much. I learned a lot from him."

At the age of 67, her father died. The loss was devastating to Monique. "Once he died, I felt like I'd just lost the world." At twelve years old, she was forced to take on the responsibility of looking after the household. Remembering that period now, Monique recalls, "I never had a childhood, because I had to grow up so fast. I was learning how to do so many things because my dad died."

Abuse Begins

Left to take care of her five children on her own, Monique's mother started drinking heavily, eventually becoming what Monique calls a "dysfunctional alcoholic." Her father left the family a generous pension from his time in the military, but, "we never saw the money cause my mother spent it all. Yeah, she would take the check and never come back until three, four days later. Even to this day, she'll buy cases of liquor and beer. Not just one or two, she buys a whole case. She still drinks really bad. As soon as she wakes up in the morning."

Monique's mother couldn't afford to stay in their apartment after her husband's death. So she took the children and bounced around, staying with friends and family for a while before finally settling in a public housing complex in Coney Island. Once they were in the projects, Monique's mother only sank deeper into alcoholism and became less and less engaged as a parent. She set few rules for the children and essentially let them look after themselves. She also had different boyfriends who would periodically stay over; Monique didn't like any of them.

She recalls one telling incident that occurred when they were in the Coney Island projects: "My sister and I, we didn't have curfews. There was a shooting like three blocks down. They was always shooting in Brooklyn. And my mother's boyfriend, he goes, 'Do you know what time it is?' It was like four in the morning and I had to go to school the next day. I'm like, 'Yeah. It's four o'clock.' 'Didn't you hear them shooting?' 'Yeah but they wasn't shooting at me!' I told him. I said, 'Well my mother said as long as we have keys and we don't have to wake her up, we can come in the house whenever we want.' At twelve, thirteen [years old], come in the house at four in the morning. Anything could have happened to us. She didn't care."

Monique's mother's favoritism of some of her children and criticism of her and her sister only intensified as she continued to drink. Eventually, the treatment turned abusive, with her mother verbally berating and regularly beating them.

Slowly, Monique's self-esteem and confidence was broken down. "I've always been thick, so my mother was like, 'Oh, you're stupid. You're fat. You're ugly. You're never going to be nothing. [I] went to camp, and at the end of camp I came home with a trophy and all these certificates. I was so proud of myself because I was thick so you know, people always make fun, 'You can't do this, you can't do that,' and she got drunk one day and she ripped them all up. So, I mean, it destroyed me.

"My mother took all her anger out on me and my other sister. I mean, extension cords, high-heeled shoes, two by fours, whatever was within her reach, we got beat with it. She even hit me so hard that I lost my eyesight for a week. I was in the hospital. First I got cross-eyed, then I couldn't see anything. So I used to get beat all the time, all the time. Child abuse wasn't a big thing back then so nobody did anything."

Another Turn for the Worse

When Monique was a young teenager, her mother started a relationship with Larry, a man who was particularly antagonistic towards Monique. Still hurting from the loss of her father, Monique was standoffish to all of the men her mother dated, but Larry was especially upsetting. He frequently tried to take on a fatherly role and one evening started yelling at Monique in front of her friends. He thought she shouldn't be allowed to have her friends over, which angered Monique, since she had completed her chores and was doing well in school. "I was like 'No, I go to school, I do what I'm supposed to do. Why can I not have company?'"

In frustration, Monique tried to push Larry out of her room by shoving her bedroom door into him. Infuriated, the twenty-nine-year-old Larry started a fistfight with fourteen-year-old Monique. Her mother's response was to kick her out of the apartment for the night. "She threw me out. My face was all bruised up."

It was late at night when a bruised Monique left the housing projects where she lived and took the city bus to her older half-brother's apartment. "I didn't remember the apartment number and I didn't want to knock on everybody's door. So I'm standing there and I'm mad and I'm crying and people are asking me 'Are you alright?' And I'm not saying nothing." Eventually Monique told a neighbor her brother's name, and she was taken to his apartment, where she spent the night.

The next day, they paid Larry a visit. "They took me out to breakfast that Saturday, with both my brothers. And they went to my mother's house and they beat the living crap out of [Larry]."

To Monique's disappointment, her mother stayed with Larry despite the incident. "How are you going to let some man come between you and your daughter? She still stayed with him though." Monique couldn't stay with her half-brother long-term and with nowhere else to live, she went back to her mother's apartment. Unfortunately, the physical fight was not the worst thing that Larry would do to Monique in the course of his relationship with her mother.

"He raped me and my sister. And he went to jail because I told. I told my mother and she was like 'It's your fault. You shouldn't be so fast.' He was already sleeping with my oldest sister—my mother didn't know that. And he raped me and my other sister. I told [about] me and my sister both. I'm like, 'No, I'm not going through this.' I was fourteen. She was twelve." Even though her mother blamed her for the rape, Monique called the police and reported the incidents. Larry went to prison for the rapes, effectively ending his relationship with their mother.

Marcus

During this same traumatic year, Monique met a boy from her neighborhood. Marcus was very sympathetic to Monique's situation with her mother, and he proved to be a positive and supportive friend. "He couldn't believe some of the things my mother used to do. He always stayed by me. Always." This relationship ultimately provided Monique with the love and support she was missing at home.

Eventually, Marcus and Monique began a romantic relationship, which became sexual when she was just fifteen. Although her mother had put her on birth control pills at age twelve, she never talked to Monique about sex or pregnancy, or even explained what the birth control pill was. "My mom never said, 'Okay, I'm going to put you on birth control pills because I don't want you to get pregnant, or I would like for you to use condoms. I'm so different with my kids. I try to talk to them about everything. You can't just put a child on something and not explain to them why you're doing it. She never really was a mother to me."

When she was sixteen, Monique became pregnant with Marcus' child; a lack of understanding of pregnancy and the pill may have caused her to take it incorrectly. Regardless, although it was unintentional, Monique was neither terribly surprised nor upset by getting pregnant, since her older sister had given birth a couple of years earlier, at the even younger age of fourteen.

Her mother initially demanded that she have an abortion. She refused, insisting that she didn't want her mother's help with the child anyhow—she and Marcus were determined to take care of their baby themselves.

Monique gave birth to her first son at sixteen and, true to her word, she and Marcus took care of him solely on their own. She was still living at home, but she refused to take any additional help from her mother, which only made her mother angrier. "I think [it] bothered my mother so much that we took care of our son. Cause [Marcus] was seventeen, I was sixteen, and he was working, I was going to school and we never asked her for a thing. We just learned how to compromise. We just grew up."

Monique stopped going to high school after her son's birth, and began attending an alternative high school equivalency program in Coney Island.[1] She had always been a good student, and she enjoyed school, but the stress of the new baby, combined with her mother's anger and abuse—which continued to escalate—made it difficult to fully concentrate on her schoolwork.

"I used to come to school with bruises and stuff and crying, like I couldn't focus in school because I had all these other things going on with me. I was good at school and stuff but because of everything else that was going on, I couldn't focus. I told my teacher and she told me about Covenant House." Covenant House provides shelter to homeless and runaway teenagers, many of whom, like Monique, are escaping abusive homes.

But Monique still wasn't quite ready to leave. Her son was still an infant, and she was still underage. Despite the abuse at

---

1. High school equivalency programs prepare students for the General Educational Development Test (GED), a certification test of high-school level academic skill.

home, she wasn't sure that she was ready to be on her own. It wasn't until her life was actually threatened and she feared her son might grow up without a mother that she finally gathered the courage to leave.

The Last Straw

Over time, Monique became nearly immune to her mother's abuse and took the regular beatings in stride. Eventually, she hardly even felt any pain. "I got beat so much growing up that this one particular day she beat me and, I mean, she was sweating and everything. [But] it wasn't hurting me. It looked like it was hurting her more than it was hurting me, because I got immune to it."

Monique's mother was in the midst of this beating when Monique calmly turned and said, "Are you finished yet?" She flew into an even bigger rage and went down the hall to her neighbor's apartment, where a drinking buddy of hers lived. Monique's mother asked her neighbor to aim a gun at Monique, and maybe even fire a shot in order to scare her back into obedience. "It was just supposed to scare me. There wasn't supposed to have been any bullets in [the gun]. The girl was even more scared than I was because it wasn't supposed to go off. So when it went off, she freaked out." Stunned, Monique left and walked down the hall to their apartment. "You know at first it didn't even hit me. So I calmly just opened the door, I walked out, I banged on the wall, cause the walls are cheap in the projects. So I'm banging on the wall, my children's dad, he opens the door, and he goes, 'What happened?' and I was more pissed because these were a brand new pair of jeans. You know. Can't fix that! There's a hole in them.

"So I'm like, 'I got shot.' He's like, 'Stop playing.' So I pull down my pants and blood was shooting out like when you open up a can of juice. And that's when I just, I fainted." The bullet had gone through both of Monique's legs. "I lost four pints of blood. They said I lost so much blood I could go into a coma."

The shooting occurred over ten years ago, but even today, when Monique talks about it, she seems stunned and shocked by the fact that her own mother would put her life in such danger. "She set me up. Had somebody shoot me with a gun when I was seventeen years old. [I] almost died. And all I kept thinking was 'Wow, my son's going to grow up without a mom.'"

The presence of Monique's young son was one of the worst aspects of the shooting, and he still bears psychological scars. "I kept hearing them yell, 'Get the baby out of here,' 'Get the baby out of here.' And he remembers so much. He was always one of those kids that was so bright, and so into everything, that . . . it traumatized him. His whole behavior changed. I had to literally take him to see a psychiatrist. He remembers so much."

Monique went to the hospital, but despite the danger that she had put her daughter in, her mother still wasn't remorseful. "Even when I got shot, I was in and out of consciousness. The first words that I heard were, 'Is she dead yet?' Those were her words, 'Is she dead yet?' I will never in my life forget that."

Monique thinks that her life was spared by divine intervention. "I came home that Friday and I went to church that Sunday, cause I said I can only give God the praise, because I knew it was Him. It was not my time to go."

At the hospital, Monique told the doctors that the shooting was an accident, and neglected to tell anyone of her mother's involvement. She was concerned for her siblings, and she knew that if she told authorities that her mother had set her up to be shot, her younger sisters and brother would be placed in foster care. "I even lied for her. If I told I would have had to tell on my mother. And I didn't want my sisters to go to foster care. I didn't want to go to foster care, cause even then I was only seventeen."

In addition to everything else, during the period that Monique was in the hospital recovering, her mother never called the GED program to tell them why she was absent. As a result, following a full week's absence, they discharged her from the program.

By this point, Monique was understandably terrified of her mother. "Even just to be in the house with her I was just so scared, like 'What's she going to try next?' So I was like, 'That's it.' And I love my son. I don't want him to have to grow up without a mom." Unfortunately, at this point Monique was still seventeen, and therefore not yet legally independent. "I stuck it out until I turned eighteen. [The shooting] happened when I was seventeen, in October. I turned eighteen in February and I left. I left. I just took enough clothes for us to wear, took all my important papers for me and my son, and I never went back. I never went back."

Even today, Monique still struggles with her abusive past. "People used to always tell me you know, 'Try to put that behind you,' and 'Move on' and stuff. And it's like really, really hard to put something like that behind you, because this was the person that almost took my life. And that's my mom. And I feel that children aren't asked to be born, that's a choice that you make. I can't help that I look like her mother."

A Fresh Start

After so many years with her abusive mother, Monique was finally on her own. She went to Covenant House, the shelter for teens her teacher had told her about. It was an ideal option for her, as it was created specifically for young women like her—young runaways and victims of abuse. "I explained things to them and they let me stay there. I didn't know anything about shelters. I went with my son and they just took us in then and there." Monique was still dating Marcus at this point, and while he continued to provide her with emotional support, he was not ready to leave home, so she went to Covenant House by herself.

Covenant House was a turning point in Monique's young life in that it provided a place for her to begin working through her anger from the years of abuse she had suffered at the hands of her mother. There, she found herself among many other teenagers who had gone through similar kinds of abuse. The support groups, counselors, and group therapy at Covenant House enabled Monique to begin working through what she had experienced as a child. "All those years of just talking about it helped me so much."

Covenant House has several locations throughout New York City. The different facilities offer different programs for their residents. Initially, Monique was placed at the facility designated for pregnant women or women with very young children. "The first Covenant House I went to was called Mother and Child, where you can be pregnant or just have a child. But that one you had to be on welfare, you had to apply for welfare so they could help you find an apartment.[2] I didn't want to be on welfare. So they had the other Covenant House, called Rights of Passage, where you worked, they take 10 percent of your money to help you save up for an apartment. So that's what I did." Monique got a job working retail at a local mall, making about eight dollars an hour.

Nearly a year after leaving home, Monique learned that she was five months pregnant. She had been visiting Marcus on the weekends, but the pregnancy came as something of a shock, since Monique was taking the birth control pill and had been menstruating regularly. Initially, Monique felt completely unprepared and considered aborting the baby. "I was like, 'Oh man. I'm really not ready to have another kid.' I was nineteen. Just like, 'I'm not ready for this.' So I went to have an abortion, I never really believed in abortion, but I was like I'm not ready for another child. But when they told me I was at twenty weeks, I was like, no, I can't. I can't do that."

Unfortunately, keeping the baby meant that Monique would have to leave Covenant House. Pregnant women were not allowed to stay in that facility and there wasn't space in the one designated for mothers and young children. The staff suggested that she apply for shelter and put her name on the waiting list for a Section 8 housing voucher.[3] With little job experience, no high school diploma, and no GED, Monique's options were limited. Clearly, she couldn't bring her young child back to her mother's

2. Welfare and public assistance are used interchangeably; both refer to the federal entitlement program Temporary Assistance for Needy Families (TANF).

3. Section 8 is a federal housing subsidy for low-income renters that pays the difference between 30 percent of the renters' incomes and the fair market rent.

violent home. Monique had little choice but to go on public assistance and enter the shelter system.

Getting Some Help

In March of 1994, five months pregnant and nineteen years old, Monique was placed in a Tier II family shelter on Staten Island.[4] The family shelter would prove to be pivotal in Monique's life. "Going into the shelter was like the best thing that happened to me. Yeah, that I believe." Four months after moving in, she gave birth to her second son.

She also thinks that the Staten Island shelter was a better place for her than Covenant House. "They had a day care for my baby. They had day care for my three year old. I took my GED, they had computers in the afternoon that I did. And then I did [a job training program]. I did my internship—reception and the mail. So I got a lot of experience. I did a lot of stuff, and they didn't have those opportunities at Covenant House."

Monique is particularly appreciative of the support she received from the shelter staff. "I had a lot of support when I lived in Staten Island. I really did. I really did. It was like a family." Monique especially liked her caseworker and felt that the staff at the shelter recognized her potential and supported her efforts. "If you was doing something good with yourself or trying, they'd work with you."

Monique also took full advantage of the programs the shelter had to offer. "I got my GED while I was there. I took up so

4. Tier II Shelters are nonprofit operated facilities for homeless families with children 18 or younger.

many different programs that they were offering." One of her favorite programs was one aimed at encouraging literacy for parents and children together. "[It] was really helpful to me because I had to read to my son, which was something I always did anyway, but even more so. We learned together—mother and son. It was so much fun, doing things together."

Monique also participated in the job training programs. The shelter staff quickly recognized her competence and aptitude, and soon she was doing secretarial work in the shelter's main office. "So they asked if I could help answer the phones and do the mail and make copies. And I was so good at it, and I picked it up like that, that they was like, 'I like her, can she stay?' I'm very good at answering the phones and messing around with computers. So they just kept me even when I graduated [from the internship program]. I stayed until I moved out. Even when I graduated, I just kept going back. It was a lot of fun. I learned so much."

Monique received her GED in December 1994. For the next six months she continued to work in the shelter's administrative offices and took care of her newborn son. When she moved out in June 1995, she left not only with her two young sons, but also with a GED, increased literacy, and work experience.

A New Home

The shelter's housing specialist helped Monique find a two-bedroom apartment in a Section 8 building in Brooklyn. Monique was collecting welfare for herself and her two young sons, and they were happy to finally have a safe place to call home. Unfortunately, in July, just one month after they moved into the new apartment, Monique fell and broke her ankle. The break was so bad, she needed multiple surgeries to place three pins into her ankle to hold it together. She couldn't walk or put weight on her ankle for months and was forced to stay home through her second surgery in October.

Monique hated being homebound and by the end of October had grown stir-crazy. She was anxious to get out of the house and hoped to start working again. "In November, I was like, I can't do this anymore. [I] went down to [the job training center], limping and everything, trying to walk in these heels. They like, 'You sure you're ready?'" Monique's job counselor sent her on an interview to work for a program within a shelter that trained women to be licensed at-home daycare providers.

Monique was hired as a business developer, making flyers, resumes, and business cards, and helping women with the elaborate application process that certification required. She started the position in December and her level of responsibility quickly increased. Eventually, she was allowed to help with the training classes and to fill in for trainers who were out sick. Now she's been working there for nearly ten years and is considered one of the most crucial staff members in her organization, routinely helping her coworkers when they have questions.

This would seem a fitting end to Monique's story. She had a home, a full-time job, and her kids were happy and healthy. But unfortunately, her experience with homelessness was not a singular one, and this is only half of Monique's story.

PART II

New Romances

Throughout this whole ordeal, Monique and Marcus had continued dating, but the relationship finally ended in 1996. Monique had become frustrated with him since he neither worked nor went to school and instead relied on his mother to take care of him. "I'm not taking care of a man. You need to get a job. I grew up, so I kind of grew out of the relationship. And he met someone who would take care of him." Marcus met a woman who was willing to provide for him in a way that Monique refused. They are now married and living in Long Island. Monique says that she and Marcus still have a close relationship. "He's a nice person and we're still the best of friends."

Although the two are friendly, Marcus has provided little emotional or financial support for his children. He only sees the children once every few months, claiming he's too busy, even though he doesn't work and only attends school one night a week. It's a sore point with Monique. "Don't give me that crap that you're too tired. Try working six days a week and taking care of four kids. I still have to go home and cook, do laundry." In addition, Monique hasn't received child support payments from him in ten years.

A month after breaking up with Marcus, Monique met Carlos, a bus driver and part-time bouncer who is twelve years her senior. At this point in her life, Monique had only ever been romantically involved with one man, Marcus. Carlos was older, had a job that put him in touch with musicians and club owners, and was a charming guy. The two started a relationship soon after they met.

Complicating matters was the fact that Marcus wasn't entirely out of the picture. Although they had broken up and Monique had begun a new relationship, Carlos's work often took him away from New York and Marcus and Monique occasionally fell back into old habits when he came to visit his children. "Marcus and I had always been friends, and he and his girlfriend had just gotten together. [But] when he would come and see the kids every now and again . . . you know . . . being together for eight years."

In 1996, Monique became pregnant again. Again she was on the birth control pill, and she insists that she and Carlos "always used protection." But after she skipped a period, she went to her doctor, who told her that she was four months into the pregnancy. Initially, Monique was sure that the baby was Carlos's. Although they had used condoms consistently, they had also been together much more frequently than she and Marcus. But the little girl that Monique gave birth to bears a strong resemblance to Marcus. They are saving up for a paternity test so they will know conclusively who the baby's father is, but in the meantime, both Marcus and Carlos look out for the little girl as if she were their daughter. "I told both of them, you know, 'things happen,' and they both take care of her . . . because neither of them have [other] daughters."

Monique continued her relationship with Carlos, and in 1999 the two had another baby, a little boy, two years after their daughter was born. Eventually, however, Monique and Carlos's relationship started to fall apart. Carlos ran with a dangerous crowd, and seemed to constantly get into trouble, or show up to meet Monique bloody and bruised. Ultimately Monique decided that his lifestyle wasn't good for her or her children. "Something is always happening to him, and I don't want someone knocking on my door pulling the bullet because they looking for him. So I had to leave him alone. He was always a hard-working man, he still is. But every time I turn around somebody cut up his neck and somebody shot at him. I mean, I have kids, and I need to live for my kids, and I can't live my life like looking behind my shoulder the whole time because someone is looking for him, so we just vowed to stay friends."

A Marriage, a Move, and a Turn for the Worse

Less than a year after giving birth to her fourth, and last, child, Monique met a man named James during a work-related trip to upstate New York. By that point, Monique's four children were getting older and their 2-bedroom Brooklyn apartment was beginning to feel cramped. "It started to get too small as my kids started getting bigger." In 2000, after dating for a year, Monique and James decided to get married. James had a daughter of his own, so there were now two adults and five children living in the 2-bedroom apartment. Between the two of them, Monique and James were able to afford a much larger apartment in the Bronx. Unfortunately the move meant leaving the Section 8 building and giving up Monique's federal housing assistance.

Sadly, the marriage would last less than a year. "Maybe like two or three months after we got married, everything just changed. I knew he smoked cigarettes, I'm not really thrilled about cigarettes, but then he started smoking weed, and I'm like, 'When did this occur?'"

James, a jealous man, was critical of Monique's children and thought that they were spoiled. Eventually he became violent. "He had a problem that my kids were so spoiled and I had so much, and how do I have so much knowing that I have four kids. Why? Cause I have four kids I can't have nice things? We got into altercations, just arguing all the time, and he broke my nose. And, you only got to hit me once. I'm not with that domestic violence. I said, 'My pride is too big, my self-esteem is too high. And it took me a long time to build up my self-esteem and I'm not going to let anybody tear it down. Nope.' I said, 'I refuse. You need to go. I refuse to be with anybody that hit me. I made it this far without you, and I'm quite sure I'll make it further without you.'"

The abuse was the beginning of a string of bad luck for Monique. In 2001, at the end of her marriage to James, she was already in a tight spot financially. She hadn't been fully paid for her maternity leave in 1999, and with strained family finances, they had fallen a little behind on their rent and utility payments. Monique was hoping to make it up with her 2001 tax refund. Unfortunately, she and James had filed their taxes for 2000 together, and since he had outstanding school loans, Monique didn't receive a tax refund, even though she and James had at that point separated. "Then they took my income tax in 2000, so I wasn't able to catch up on it, and there is only so much time that they let you stay there without catching up on the rent that you owe."

To top it all off, the apartment was old and one day they came home from a weekend out of town to find that the pipes had burst and their bathroom ceiling caved in. "We was on vacation and the fire department had to come and tear down my door, because the water was leaking downstairs. We wasn't home, and they had to turn off the water pipe and fix that. And they told us, it doesn't matter how many times they fix it, unless they put new wiring stuff in it, it's just going to keep happening. So I was like, I can't deal with this, I have kids, so we left."

Homeless Again

At this point, Monique found herself in a bizarre situation. She was working full-time at a shelter for homeless women and children, and she herself was now a homeless single mother of four. Clearly, she knew the procedure well, and knew what the next step would have to be, but after hearing so many nightmarish stories about the Emergency Assistance Unit (EAU), she was very reluctant to go.[5] Instead, Monique's best friend generously offered to let her and her four children stay with them. There were no extra bedrooms, so Monique's family slept on the living room floor. Monique was hoping that during that period she would be able to save enough money for a new apartment, which ultimately she wasn't able to do. "I had to give her money, just to stay there, plus help her buy food, so I was never really able to save up any money."

Monique and her four children stayed on her friend's living room floor from July until October, when it began to get cold and the children had to play inside. Monique decided it was finally time to do what she'd been dreading. She had been on the waiting list for a Section 8 housing voucher for ten years, and still hadn't received one. "They take too long. I just had no shame. I'm like

5. The Emergency Assistance Unit is the gateway to the City shelter system.

this is the only way I know I'm going to get Section 8. I need a 3 bedroom, and I can't afford to pay $1,400 by myself." So, Monique told her children what they were about to do, and took the family to the EAU in the Bronx. "It was really hard. To my kids, I explained what EAU was about, and I said, 'We have to work together as a team, but we can do this.' And that's what we did."

The trip to the EAU began a three-month period of nearly constant transition for Monique and her kids. The family was denied shelter three times. On each occasion, they went through a protracted period of overnight shelter placements, assessment periods which often stretched much longer than the intended ten days, and multiple rounds of questioning.[6] "You stay for 10 days, they find you ineligible, you go back to the EAU. They do overnights, they place you somewhere else. You keep doing the same things."

EAU staff was convinced that Monique could take her children to live in James's mother's three-bedroom apartment in a housing project, where James was living as well. When Monique explained that not only were they separated, but that he was also violent towards her, they told her she needed to get a court order to prove that he was abusive, and maintained that she was ineligible for shelter because she could go to her former mother-in-law's apartment.

Throughout this process, Monique continued to work

---

6. The application for shelter involves a 10-day assessment period during which families stay in a conditional placement. While applying for shelter at the Emergency Assistance Unit (EAU) or the Prevention Assistance and Temporary Housing (PATH) intake center families are required to rpovide the names and addresses of all residences from the two years preceding homelessness. Caseworkers then call or visit these residences to determine whether or not families may return there. Despite 10-day limits, assessment periods can, and often do, last for weeks.

full-time, spending each evening picking her children up from school, and then going to the EAU to lobby for acceptance into the shelter system. "[I] still came to work. EAU is open twenty-four hours. You go in the evening, and they give you passes in the morning. They only give you eight-hour passes, but I would call, say, 'Look, I work.' And they would extend it two hours, so I could go pick my kids up from day care, and then take them back to the EAU. It just makes the process longer when you're not there all day, but I wasn't trying to quit my job just cause we was [homeless]."

In January, after nearly three months of back-and-forth trips to the EAU, Monique decided to give up and take her children back to her friend's apartment. The decision was made in part because all four of her children became ill with what Monique thinks was food poisoning from the food at the EAU. "My kids got sick and I gave up. So I went back to my friend's house. EAU is disgusting. All four of my kids ended up with a stomach virus. My youngest child got it first, he was throwing up, he had the runs, and my daughter got it, and my two older boys. It was a mess, I was like, 'Oh, I can't do this.'"

Monique and the kids moved back in with her friend and resumed sleeping on the living room floor. They stayed there from January until October, at which point Monique decided to go back to the EAU and try again. She was very hesitant to go back, but saw it as a necessary step. "I just said, 'We have to do this.'"

Back to the EAU

After her prior experience at the EAU, Monique knew to

do a few things differently. First, she took their own food. "I said, 'I don't want you eating anything from there. I don't want you running around playing with the little kids cause I don't want you guys getting sick.' And I said 'We already know what to expect.' And we did it."

Monique also marked "unknown" when asked for James's current address. She didn't want to have to go through the same argument about living in her former mother-in-law's apartment. This time, Monique and her children were accepted into the system on their first application. It took a few days to find a space appropriate for a family with three boys and one girl, but after a week, Monique and the kids were placed in a facility called Mike's House.

What followed was a ten-month period during which Monique lived in one shelter and worked in another. In a way, her job at the Bronx shelter proved helpful during this period. She had friends who were caseworkers and housing specialists, and when she was appointed a young, inexperienced caseworker at Mike's House, she was able to get better advice and help from her friends at work. At one point, her caseworker told her that in order to get housing assistance, she would have to quit her job, which Monique knew wasn't true. So, with advice from coworkers, Monique started acting as her own caseworker. "I was just pretty much doing everything on my own."

Apart from some close friends at work, Monique kept her situation a secret. "I'm very private about things, I don't go around telling anyone my business anyway. I told one caseworker and the housing specialist, cause I needed help. And the caseworker [at

Mike's House] didn't know what she was doing."

Monique was extremely proud of how well her kids coped with their situation. They didn't complain, and tried not to put added stress on their mother. Still, it was a tough period for the whole family. "It's a process. And it's harder when you got lots of kids, and your kids are older. When they [are] younger they don't really understand, they don't care. But you know I told them, 'This is the only way we can get a three bedroom, and get help with me paying the rent. It's two to a room, so at least you can come and go, you get your own keys.' So you know, we really dealt with it. They worked really hard, helping me out with little things. We worked really well as a team."

Luckily, in the summer of 2003, Monique was approved for a Section 8 federal housing voucher. She had been on the waiting list since 1993, but ultimately received the voucher because she was applying from a homeless shelter. Monique immediately started looking for an apartment. "I went down there on my lunch break, picked up my voucher, and started calling. It was like, I'm not playing, I'm trying to get up out of here, I don't want to spend another Christmas in a shelter." She and her four children moved into a three-bedroom apartment in the Bronx, closer to the center where Monique runs her training programs.

Today

Monique has been working for the day care training program since 1995. At this point, she is one of the senior staff members and has myriad responsibilities. "Most people, even my coworkers, they'll ask me if they don't know, because I've been here for so long." Monique loves her position, and even works on the weekends at a different center that helps women get re-certified to run their day care centers. "I love it so much I do it on the weekends."

The center is housed in a shelter for homeless families, and the program is free for currently or formerly homeless women who live or have lived in any shelter in New York City. Monique is active in encouraging the shelter residents to take part in the class, even if they don't want to run day care centers. "Even if you don't want to do this, it can help you with your children—learning how to talk to them, learning how to deal with them, [learning] why children do certain things when they're at a certain age. You would have that understanding instead of getting mad all the time and cursing at them, like, 'Oh, they're doing this because they're two.' So I get a lot of people to come. But a lot of people take [the course] because they really want to do something, like they want to do something when they move out of here."

Monique takes her responsibilities at work very seriously. Partly because she herself was in a shelter, she understands how valuable the recognition of small accomplishments can be. "I take this so seriously. I do things a little bit different than my coworkers and because I'm computer literate. So I make perfect attendance certificates. I make achievement awards. Who got the highest score on a test. I do so many different kinds of certificates for them. I give them little things that say 'Graduation' on it. Yeah, because it's something special. Most of the people I get are really into this. This is something they really want to do. They try their best. So, I make graduation fun."

Part of Monique's job is to help train the day care providers to pay attention to signs that a child might be the victim of abuse. Again, given her background, Monique takes this responsibility very seriously. Some of the other trainers at the center allow women to graduate as long as they have missed fewer than three classes. For Monique, if a woman misses a class on Sudden Infant Death Syndrome (SIDS), shaken baby syndrome, or child abuse, she refuses to let them graduate. She understands the seriousness of these issues on a level that other trainers might not. "I always apologize when it comes to SIDS, shaken baby syndrome, and child abuse because you don't know what people have gone through and sometimes it can, you know, touch them in a way, like especially if they've gone through it, [it could] bring back memories so I always apologize for those three classes. We know that it happens. I know that it happens because that's how my life was. You know, a lot of people don't know how to look for the signs, what to do. I take this very seriously."

Today, Monique has no relationship with her mother, who has never apologized, or acknowledged abusing Monique and arranging for her to be shot. Likewise, her children effectively have no relationship with their grandmother. "I've never asked her for anything. Not even to this day. She has never bought my son anything and he's thirteen. Nothing. Not a t-shirt. Not no socks." Monique did, however, meet a woman at work who has become a surrogate mother to her and grandmother to her children, who call her 'Nana.' "That's who I see as a mom. Like when I have problems I talk to her. Cause I never had that relationship with my mother."

Monique is close to her younger siblings, particularly her little brother. Unfortunately, the sister who was also abused by their mother has never fully recovered. "She still hasn't gotten it together. Like her life traumatized her. She's just not strong. I had a lot of people in my life that just changed me, made me see that there are other things out there. You don't have to just settle. Now, I'm not settling for anything less than the best. I had some guidance in my life. Like, 'No, you don't need to do that. Why don't you try this?' And I was always one that would listen. I would just hear what you're saying. I might not do it at that moment, but eventually it sinks in. So my sister's like the opposite. She lost her kids. She still hasn't gotten herself together. And I refuse to be like that."

Although Monique is still struggling to come to terms with her mother's abuse, she has made huge efforts to ensure that she's a better parent than her mother was. She has worked hard to learn how to be loving and supportive, particularly with her first child, who witnessed Monique's abuse. "I had to learn how to communicate with him. I had to learn how to tell him I love him, you know, to hug him. Because those things wasn't done to me."

Monique's oldest son is her only child with any memory of his grandmother. Although he was very young, he remembers the violence. Monique encourages him to try to put these memories aside and focus on the future. "He can remember even when he was like three. He'll come and say, 'Mom, do you remember when Grandma did . . . ' you know, and I'm like, 'You remember that?' Yeah, that boy has a very good memory. He remembers so much. But I told him, 'Don't let it bother you. It doesn't bother me.' I've learned to put that behind me and just move on with my life."

She also sent her oldest son to a psychiatrist to help him work through his memories of his mother's abuse. The treatment involved both individual sessions and family sessions, which Monique credits with helping her learn how to be closer to her children. "That's what I always wanted, to be close to my kids. And that was something I had to learn. So when my son went to the psychiatrist, they had the days where they saw him one on one. And they had the days where they saw us together as a family. So it's like now we're the best of friends. Me and all four of my children are the best of friends."

Looking Forward and Learning from the Past

Monique has managed to find a way to look at her past and the abuse she suffered in a positive light. She was ultimately motivated by her desire to prove her mother wrong. "I always said that I'm going to make my mother a liar, that I am going to be somebody. I am going to do something with my life and I'm going to be a better mother than she ever was. So it just made me stronger.

"I used to cry all the time just to talk about it. But now I've been through it for so long, and talked about it so much, that it doesn't bother me as much anymore. I feel that I've come a long way because of everything that's happened to me.

"I teach my children to stand up for what you believe in, be proud of who you are and where you came from. And the things that happened to me, I think pretty much made me stronger. I'm more eager to do this. I really want to prove to people that I can do this. And I refuse to settle for anything less. That's what makes life grand. Life is a learning process. And it's a game. My game ain't over yet. Not even close."

Today, Monique leads a program in New York City shelters that provides women with certification to run day care in their own homes. The training is free for shelter residents and it enables women to exit the shelter with the tools for self-employment. It is further beneficial in that it provides women with an alternative to expensive day care options for their own children. After being subjected to so much abuse for such a long period, Monique is especially grateful for the opportunity to ensure that thousands of young children across the city are in safe, happy, home environments, with well-trained people keeping careful watch over them.

CONCLUSION

These six stories show resilience, strength, and incredible optimism in the face of nearly insurmountable odds. The men and women profiled here managed to pull positive outcomes from the most challenging period of their lives. They acquired new skills, kicked bad habits, sought out higher levels of education, and ultimately stabilized and motivated themselves and their families.

For each of these stories, there are scores more that demonstrate similar fortitude. But there are also many others that do not end so positively. Every year thousands of children and families become trapped in the cycle of homelessness and poverty. Many of them don't have access to the types of programs and supportive services that were made available to Theresa, Shelly, Belle, Angela, Andre, and Monique. Without this kind of support, some families simply do not have the necessary skills to pull themselves up and out of homelessness, and they are unable to turn dependency into self-sufficiency.

These stories have also demonstrated systemic failures throughout New York's homeless services system. We have seen that the process at the Emergency Assistance Unit fails time and time again. Children become ill, women are told to live with their abusive spouses or alcoholic relatives, and families are unfairly denied shelter and support.

In 2004, the City moved to correct the situation. The Department of Homeless Services created the Prevention Assistance and Temporary Housing (PATH) intake center, a new facility for homeless families applying for shelter, and the Housing Stability Plus program, a new rental assistance subsidy intended to expedite the move to permanent housing—two extremely positive steps.

These stories, and so many more, demonstrate that what is needed to solve the homeless epidemic is a real commitment to providing services and support to these families in need. Then, and only then, will we make significant strides in the battle to end family homelessness once and for all.